AF343537

ELITE AGENT

Nora Lakheal
In collaboration with Bertrand Ferrier

ELITE ZGENT
THE INSPIRING STORY OF A WOMAN
IN THE INTELLIGENCE SERVICE

To my father.

Max Milo, Paris, 2023
www.maxmilo.com
ISBN : 978-2-31501-254-1

Float like a butterfly.
Sting like a bee.

(Floats like a butterfly.
Stings like a bee).

Mohamed Ali

Prologue

It's time to go.

After many months of shadowing and surveillance, our superiors have decided to tighten the net around Nasser and his companions. He is a terrorist released from prison less than two years ago; two of his relatives have just returned from a two-month stay in Pakistan. Today's objective: to break into the apartment of the main suspect. While the specialists install the technical surveillance equipment, with my colleagues in support, I'll be in charge of checking Nasser's comings and goings, to make sure he doesn't return home too soon.

We gather in the courtyard of our base lodge and divide into two vehicles. One for the technicians. One for the operatives, tasked with ensuring their safety and tracking down the suspect.

I take my place aboard the second. Yacouba drives it. He drops me off a hundred meters from the mosque. We all take up our positions. We test our radios. I say a *quick* prayer:

- My God, please don't let me lose it, *inch'allah ya rabbi*!

Preserving civil peace and freeing my religion from extremist criminals are among the main reasons why I became a General Intelligence agent in the "Islam group" of the Section Opérationnelle et Recherche Spécialisée, or SORS.

In the earpiece, a voice:

- To all, from Yacouba, the lens has just left his home. He's heading for the mosque. Nora, get ready.

- From Nora to Yacouba, received.

The minutes that follow are sticky.

Collantes.

Endless.

To the point of relief, as it were:

- From Nora to all, I have Nasser in my sights. I'll take it.

He stands before me, our precious one. We've been at his heels for so many months now!

I know him by heart. No woman in her life has looked at him, stared at him or scrutinized him as much as I have. I think about him all the time. I want to know everything about his activities, his schedule, his preferences and his plans. My life revolves around him. Exclusively. Depending on what he's up to, I can go weeks without a day off, get up at 5.30 in the morning to follow him to the mosque, wear a veil from head to toe or dress up as a midget - nothing is out of the question as long as I'm likely to pick up information which, in turn, could convince our bosses that we have enough evidence to bring him in for questioning.

Nasser is tall. Very slim. Balding head. He's not old, yet he *looks* old. His long beard flutters in the breeze. He walks towards the mosque. He seems to be mumbling to himself. A habit with him. He enters the place of worship. I warn my colleagues that he has just been joined by his two companions, Marvin and Abdelkrim, who have just returned from Pakistan.

- From Jean-Baptiste to all: effective penetration. We need twenty minutes after this top.

Ten minutes tick by. The targets must be praying. Without missing a beat, I keep my eyes on the entrance to the mosque, tense at the thought that my colleagues' lives are in my hands. Suddenly, I see my three objectives appear... and fork. I announce the news: the man is not heading home. With Marvin and Abdelkrim, he's making good time.

- From Nora, we head for the Mona Lisa.

La Joconde is Marvin's place of residence. Above all, it's a low-income housing estate, making it one of the worst settings for a shadowing operation. Entering a complex of this type without being one of its inhabitants is a virtual guarantee of being destroyed in no time. Leaving, I stay back, although close enough to see Marvin taking Abdelkrim and Nasser towards a group of young people hanging out at the bottom of Tower B. It's September. The weather is fine. Nasser seems happy and at ease among the twenty-somethings around him.

Then Abdelkrim beckons his companions to follow him into the A-bar. Immediately afterwards, he turns and looks around. A security move, no doubt. The man is suspicious. He meets my gaze. I lower my eyes immediately. I hope he hasn't spotted me or memorized me! I prefer to think he hasn't - unlikely. It all happened in a flash. This is no time to be found out...

The trio climb Tower A. I let a couple of minutes elapse before climbing in behind them. After checking that the hall is empty, I stop in front of the mailboxes. I spot Abdelkrim's name, take a photo of the block of boxes and get out without delay. I'm barely outside when Nasser reappears with Marvin, bag in hand. I inform my colleagues.

- From the commander to all: operation completed, we lift the dispo. Yak, you pick up Nora. We'll be back with the techs.

- Where are you, Nora?

- To the Mona Lisa. I walk up Lion's Alley.

- Don't move, I'm coming.

- It's okay, I keep them in sight.

- It's over, Nora! F-i-n-i!

- No.

- What do you mean, "no"?

- Nasser went to Abdelkrim's with Marvin. He left with Marvin and a bag. We need to know more.

- Nora, for God's sake, you know what the boss is like when you…

- Where are you?

- There, I see you, on your right.

- Hurry, they've just been picked up in a gray 206. We follow them. When I get into the car, Yacouba sighs and says:

- You're going to get us in trouble, Nora!

- But no, we just check a little something and tear ourselves away.

- Oh, boy! Amine's driving.

- The guy we stalked in Montparnasse?

- In person! I saw his file go by. It's a big one. He's been convicted of conspiracy to commit terrorism. Normally, he lives on the other side of town. What's he doing with those two?

- You see, was I right or not?

- Well, did you get the plate?

- Yes.

- Then we're going home.

- Huh?

Yak brakes gently because the light has just turned red, and he looks me straight in the eye:

- Nora, we don't play with these louts. We're pros. A job of this calibre can't be improvised. We've got all the information we need, and we're going back to the lodge to take a puff from the captain. That'll do for today.

I bite my lip. I'm angry, but I know my partner is right. He is reason, I am ardor. He is technique, I am intuition. He is experience, I am energy. Our complementarity makes us effective. Although I know that, in a matter of seconds, overdoing it can ruin a long-term mission, I still have to learn how to channel my desire to track down criminals.

Not illogical. I've been a full peacekeeper for barely five years now, and I was never destined to wear the uniform or become an intelligence officer in the service of the French Republic.

On the contrary.

PART ONE

The Philosopher of Barbès

1.

My life changed for the first time in 1995.

I'm twenty-one years old. My path is clear. From what I've been told, I'm to marry a very wealthy Tunisian businessman specializing in construction. The man I'm to marry happens to be close to my father. My family is reassured. I'm going to be set up with someone I trust. The family friend will keep me out of trouble forever. What parent worth their salt would reject such a prospect? Aware of what's at stake for the family, and knowing that this is how it's been done in France and Tunisia for centuries, I try to find it normal, even in 1995.

In other words, I take the news in stride and, as far as I can, I try to play along, as my brain is working on the turbine. Eventually, it puts together the scattered elements that are running through my head:

- I'm not attracted to the guy,

- I don't like the idea of a husband and a narrow life plan being imposed on me, no matter how bright my future might be as a result, and I don't like the idea of a husband and a narrow life plan being imposed on me, no matter how bright my future might be as a result.

- I don't want that kind of destiny - or rather, I feel that such an existence, however respectable it may be, is not suited to my temperament.

In the end, my brain makes the decision.

In 1996, when I was in my second year of DEUG (now L2), I changed my mind and said no to this marriage project.

In spite of themselves, my parents understand that insisting would be futile. Since we're civilized people, they don't force me to obey them. On the other hand, they feel betrayed, and so they urge me to leave home. According to them, it's the next logical step. I want to be free? Fine. Do I want to waste my time studying useless things? I have to take responsibility. Out, miss Nora!

Incredulous, I didn't move. As a result, from one day to the next, I'm an outcast. When I go home - well, to Mom and Dad's, the nuance is now obvious - nobody talks to me. Only my brother, Malik, seems worthy of interest in *our* parents' eyes. With no one making an effort, I can no longer study in the 25 m² we live in. And an incessant refrain anticipates the recriminations I brood over without formulating them:

- Well, if you're not happy, just leave!

Hearing this antiphon slapping my ears and knotting my heart, I speak to the shrink who's been treating me for the past six months. Her diagnosis was without appeal:

- Nora, we have *to* go.

Once again, my brain turbines and solves the equation. On the one hand, the security of a roof and a plate. On the other, the impossibility of living together. When I put it like that, I realize that, whatever the risks, I have no choice but *to* leave.

So I go to the CROUS to look for an available room. Just then, an advert arrives. A couple is offering a room to a student in exchange for looking after their child after school. The *deal* seemed more than reasonable. Except that, in the heat of the moment, I realize a little too late that the apartment is more than three quarters of an hour from where the owners live. Three quarters of an hour out, three quarters of an hour back. In other words, an hour and a half wasted from Monday to Friday. Seven and a half hours lost per week. And, as a result, almost every day I'm guaranteed to get "home" at impossible hours.

Paradoxically, this unenviable experience galvanizes me. I've already realized that I can only grow through adversity. This is a new illustration. Fighting saves me. Even if this obligation to fight against difficulties sometimes exhausts me, it's what allows me to choose when faced with dilemmas such as: either I let myself sink, or I transcend what happens to me to move forward.

I don't want to sink. I won't let myself sink. I won't. Not in my blood.

Fighting spirit helps me to face the worst situations... and the many bad encounters I have. Evil people have a perverse gift - which they no doubt deem exceptional or sublime - for spotting young girls who are a little lost. More than one has crossed my path, adding fuel to the fire of my confusion. It was enough to destabilize me at the time, perhaps, but *in the end*, it was enough to strengthen me. Because these encounters pushed me to assert myself and, whatever the cost, to draw something positive from these traumatic experiences. I have no choice. I don't want to be annihilated. I want to move on.

Not being Superwoman, I rely on my college friends and my psychoanalyst, who sees me twice a week... for twenty-five francs a session, because she knows that every penny I have is counted. Without ever playing the guru, my therapist, lucid and encouraging, is essential to my life. She keeps telling me that I'm a good person, that I'll find myself and that I mustn't give up. Her mantra sustains me, but doesn't change the stupid, accounting reality that pursues me: I have no money. So, to my studies and childcare, I have to add part-time jobs. As luck would have it, I'm working in the canteens of Parisian hospitals. My aim is to find money, quickly and well, so that I can eat; and this is not the worst option I've been offered.

But it's still not enough. I'm hungry every day. I weigh 48 kg. I don't look like much anymore. I'm discovering what real hunger is. Several days a week, I don't eat, except when I'm lucky enough to get a snack from the family of the little boy I look after. When I have three pennies in my pocket and I pass a food store, I hesitate to go in because I know that, if I buy something now, I'll eat it... and, come evening, I'll have nothing left to eat. As someone who likes to face adversity, I'm well served. To the point of asking myself questions like: is the path I've chosen the right one? is it viable? and is it the right one?

This kind of questioning has dogged me since childhood. Worse still, it's this questioning that made me persevere in my studies of philosophy, despite the incredulous mockery of those closest to me. I can't stand it, but here's the naked truth: I've always wondered about my surroundings, the meaning of my life and my usefulness. What am I good for? What do I do? I've got the light, but so what? How can thinking, reflecting and questioning help me change the world? That's what guides me.

Very early on, I was sensitive to the voluntarist and articulate discourse of the Jeunesses Communistes, which recruited around Parisian high schools at the time. Thanks to these influences, I read Karl Marx. And I was fascinated by this strong, complex, euphoric idea of the need to redistribute wealth equitably. From then on, I saw philosophy as a perspective that could help me understand myself better and ultimately influence the way things are. Not just intellectually. In real life too.

Changing the world to share more fairly: this demand - which is a hope for many - will never leave me. I will reformulate it. I may erase the excesses, the clumsiness, the outdated phraseologies. But I will retain its lessons. Despite the mistakes, the excesses and the clashes, the question of injustice, inequality and imbalance is still with me today. And I continue to draw on this unease to combat prejudice, racism and hatred. Yes, I'm not sure I've changed much since then!

This notwithstanding, at the time, in my parents' eyes, my choice to study philosophy was incomprehensible or *at the very least* incongruous. If you're going to go to college, you might as well specialize in something useful and lucrative. Law, for example. Law is good. It's full of opportunities (what a horrible word, except for a plumber, perhaps...). Philosophy, on the other hand, is useless. You can't *do* anything with a philosophy degree. What's more, a philosopher is reputed to denigrate religion. By going down this road, Nora-la-rebelle can only become yet another example of an apostate and turn into Nora-la-mécréante!

And yet, the question of religion has always bothered me. Not because of my parents, who aren't religious. We're traditional Muslims: from a very early age, I've known what the Koran is, but not much more. Nevertheless, very early on, I clung to God. Who else could save me? My childhood was very difficult. Family tensions and lack of money left their mark on me. I believed in

God because he was the only one who could help me. What better reason could there be? What better hope?

As for the rest, as much of a "Nora Lakheal" as I am, with all that that entails in terms of representations and imagination, in terms of religious practice and spiritual foundations, I don't have much material at home. My father doesn't pray five times a day in the direction of Mecca. My mother is not veiled up to her eyes. Goodbye, clichés and conventions! To tell the truth, I only discovered the depth and vitality of religion when I discovered philosophy. My encounter with the writings of Friedrich Nietzsche was a revelation and an astonishment. Reflecting on the idea that "God is dead" grabbed me instantly and continues to titillate me on a daily basis... because this devilishly seductive assertion is at odds with everything I feel!

The truth is, I see religion like love: it falls on you without you understanding why. You can't argue with love and religion. As for me, I don't argue with the obvious. I'll always believe in God. Whatever happens, religion will be an integral part of my life. But in what form?

At this stage, I don't know. What I do know is that believing has saved me since childhood. Believing also saves me when, as a starving student, I try to avoid bakeries so as not to contemplate what I can't afford and think even harder about the hunger I'm feeling.

In short, in 1995, I'm in pretty bad shape, but I can count on three saviors - not too many, as they have their work cut out for them: psychoanalysis, God and boxing.

2.

Boxing is in the Lakheal DNA. It's *the* family sport. In his category, my uncle was amateur champion in Tunisia, where the average level is very high. Even if not every Lakheal has won a title, everyone practices the art... or rather, all the boys do. So, as soon as I left my parents, I decided to do what no self-respecting Lakheal would dare: even though I'm a woman, I joined a boxing club.

It's time. Time for me to do (a bit of) what I want. Time too for me to find an outlet to let off steam. Time for me to show my family what I'm worth, even in a field that the women in our family haven't explored.

To add another layer to this provocation, I decide to practice at the Laumière gym, in the club where my brother is registered; and, as I'm not a follower, I disdain the English boxing my family favors, and opt for savate. As I enter the gym, my head and body are buzzing. It's not easy to box on an empty stomach, but never mind! I'm overexcited at the idea of symbolically measuring myself against all the Lakheals who have preceded me on the path of combat sports. I know that I can do it, that I need to do it, and that our family, past and present, will be forced to recognize the obvious: I'm both one of them... and different.

This decision to start boxing is a great relief, but not primarily. Above all, it was a vital necessity. At the time, my life was just a series of constraints. I had to

- to keep a child off the streets;

- earn money to survive;

- take courses; and

- learn as you should.

No leisure activities on the horizon.

No encouraging prospects.

No breathing.

Just: work to live, and live to study. Aware that I'm suffocating, the psychoanalyst also encourages me in this direction.

- I'm sure it'll help to hit a bag," she announces. What's more, it might save you from inventing illnesses and somatizing.

So I'm off.

At 8pm, I'm standing outside the Laumière gymnasium. I have a strange feeling of being in a new world. I grew up between Gare du Nord and Barbès, a quarter-hour metro ride from the gym. Yet I'm no longer in my familiar space. I have no landmarks here. I remember a sociology class in which we were told that children from the underprivileged social classes never leave their neighborhoods. I guess there's some truth to some of those clichés.

The owner of the English club is Jacky Chiche. He's a Sephardic man with a reputation for glibness. When he arrives, the English boxers who had been lining up at the entrance, mostly golgoths and overwhelmingly men, enter en masse. Among them, a handsome fellow whom I take a moment to identify as David - aka Roméo - Sarfaty. The Nicolas from *Une famille formidable*, the Louis from *Sous le soleil, in* short, television's apollon smiles at me. Immediately, I stammer three words incomprehensible even to myself, and look down. Stuck in my asphyxiating daily routine, I'm no longer used to the smile of a handsome boy. Confidence has deserted me.

Instead, I cling to my willpower, which is nourished by a few inspirational figures. Muhammad Ali, for example. Rocky, of course. People who start from nothing and become something. Even if Tony Montana comes to a tragic end, I don't care! I completely identify with his character in Scarface. When he lets go:

- My hands were made for gold, and they're dipped in shit,

I feel like he's my spokesman. Maybe he and I don't put the same meaning into the idea of "gold", but what does it matter? He wants to be rich, with all that goes with it. Me, I want to extricate myself from my condition as the daughter of underprivileged immigrants. I want to break through the social barriers that stand in my way, shatter the glass and iron ceilings that suffocate me, find the ladders that will take me higher. I want to take my family with me. And let's face it: I want to do this so that, at last, my father will be proud of me.

My project is as vague as it is titanic. I don't know how I'm going to achieve it, or what it's going to be made of. So I need these characters, real or imaginary, who let me believe in the possibility of rising from nothingness through pugnacity and perseverance. If they've achieved their goals, even if only in fiction (Mohamed Ali is real!), then I can too.

In hindsight, the funny thing is that I share the same references with the big delinquents I'll have to deal with later on. They too, even younger than me, often admire Rocky and Tony Montana.

They too have their hands in the shit and, one day, decided they were better than that. They too thrill to the thought of these immigrant figures who aren't afraid of their ambitions, who believe in their dreams and fight to achieve them. On the other hand, like Tony Montana, they don't have the same definition of gold as I do. Knowing why we didn't follow the same paths, and why our goals turned out to be so different, is such a huge question that I don't want to answer it definitively; but, sometimes, I do take the time to think about it...

In 1995, at Laumière, you don't think about it. You warm up, do your scales, work on sequences, get your cardio pumping by pounding a bag with your fists and feet, and then confront each other. My first instinct is right: I discover that this sport is *my* sport. How could I have gone so long without practising it?

For a year, I come twice a week to follow Aymeric's advice. It's far away (fifty minutes from home), it's exhausting, it's sometimes painful, but it's essential. I cling to French boxing like an apneist's lungs cling to the idea that, soon, the air will replenish them. Every Monday, every Wednesday, I return with enthusiasm. Discipline, control, the ability to take and respond, the obligation to surpass oneself in order to remain dignified are all indispensable qualities that I work on and develop (or try to develop) when I come to train. Not that this impresses the *coach*, who seems to take great pleasure in nagging me at every session to the tune of :

- For God's sake, stop dancing, Nora! What's with the chick punch? You've got no guts, poor thing. Are you sure you haven't got the wrong address?

Even if poking novices in the eye is his technique for encouraging them to go further, again and again, it pisses me off that this guy is picking on me. I just give him a hateful look that tries to say: "If you knew where I came from, you poor loser, you'd talk to me differently!" I grew up with violence and contempt, so I'm not going to be impressed by a Musclor in tight tights. Yes, in skin-tight tights, because the attire of French boxers is utterly ridiculous. When you see them, you can almost hear the opening credits of Les *Brigades du tigre*, where the mustachioed cops practice savate to the tune of Henri Djian and Claude Bolling sung by Philippe Clay:

Incognito, your cops are now brains,
Neither big nor fat, they left their bikes, their horses (…).
M'sieur Clémenceau, it's no longer fair, it's the death of work!

Then, one day in 1996, the moment I'd been waiting for so impatiently arrived. At the end of class, when the moment of "free assault" arrives, I hear the phrase I've been dreaming of for months:

- Nora, are you coming with me?

Aymeric suggests I spank him in public! Without even answering, I put on my mouthguard and become SuperNora. I'm going to be ruthless. Over the months, I've trained myself to force him to swallow his superior airs and cookie-cutter formulas. The dancing chick will reveal her fire-breathing dragoness soul. Yes, this is my moment. The trainer is going to understand the cost of provoking the little girl all session long. I'm going to hit her with a few right hands and restore my dignity. I've got two minutes for that.

In *warrior* mode, I pounced on him as soon as the gong rang. Spinning dodges, blocking, Aymeric's *vista thwarts* my first attempts. Do you think I'm upset? On the contrary! The fury transcends me. I'm sure that, by persevering, I'll tire him out and find the right opening. So I multiply the raging series. Taking advantage of the fact that I've discovered myself, a right to the face brings me back to my senses.

The end of playtime has come.

While I'm still reeling from the first big jab, a chasing kick pushes me back into the ropes. A rain of fists descends on me. Right-left jabs, short hooks and uppercuts shake me. Reflexively, I try to pivot so as not to get stuck in the ropes. Soon, I'm reduced to sweeping the ring. Aymeric only lets me get out of the way to punish me. Whenever he decides, a whip is enough to put me back in the corner, where my opponent's power and stamina leave me no chance. In five words, I lived through two horrible minutes.

Saved (or almost) by the bell, I remain knocked out on my feet, incredulous and unable to move for long seconds. I'm stunned. How could I have taken such a beating? Thinking positively, I try to be proud that I didn't fall, although I'm aware that I escaped this humiliation because the *coach* chose to avoid it. Above all, I'm trying to understand what happened to me. It's been a while since I took such a severe beating. I was about to punish the unbearable Aymeric, I was sure to show who Nora is, but I was crushed in every area. So I took off my mouthguard and, jaws clenched, stepped out of the ring, my head still full of cottony clouds. I'm heading for the showers... when my tormentor calls out to me:

- What's with the long face? Are you sulking?

- Nah, I don't care. It was an assault like that, not Joe Frazer versus Muhammad Ali.

- Oh, no, you don't! I don't want to hear any more of this bullshit, Nora, do you take note? Never again! Everything depends on each assault, absolutely everything. If you don't pull your guts out as soon as you're between sixteen ropes, if you don't give more than you've got, you can stay home, there's no point in coming here. Do you understand me? I want to see your guts, you hear me? All your guts! That's what interests me about you. And, tonight, I've barely seen a gut...

- Still, that little hose didn't flinch. Did it?

- Listen, exceptionally, I'm going to be nice to you. I'm going to tell you that you've done pretty well for a dancer. Your big problem is that you don't yet have the eye of the tiger. That's something you have to work on every time you practice.

Once again, I take it. And just as I'm about to go on my way, Aymeric says:

- That said, it wasn't too bad for a start. Go on, take a shower and have a drink with us. It'll clear your head.

I stiffen up. For the past year, I've been dreading it and avoiding it. I know that getting together with the Great Guru is something most of the boys in the group look forward to. As for me, going for a drink with a clique I have nothing to say to is not my absolute dream. Except that refusing is out of the question. I'm sure that's what Aymeric's waiting for: for the humiliated chick to run off home grumbling. I won't give him that gift. Not the house style. Leaving, I just shrug my shoulders and grumble:

- OK, where to?

- At the Jaurès. When you're all dolled up, wait for us in front of the gym. We'll go in groups.

With my brain still lapping between mists and blurs, I slip underwater, unaware that, by accepting the trainer's invitation, my life has once again been turned upside down - and, this time, for good.

3.

That evening, outside the Laumière gymnasium, I waited patiently for the coach and his admirers to join me, so that I could join them in the local bar. To pass the time, I contemplate my shadow on the ground. Is it really my shadow, by the way? It seems too big. Unsuited to who I am, or think I am. No wonder: even when I look in the mirror, I don't recognize myself. I don't inhabit my body. Too hungry for it. Too many questions. Too many concerns. Too many uncertainties. So I don't feel like going out for a drink. I'm not in the mood. Especially as I'm not sure I'll be able to afford the de rigueur beer. Perhaps a Coke will be available? I don't want to embarrass myself by asking for the missing pennies...

The Great Guru puts me out of my thoughts when he finally arrives, surrounded by his mob of *fans*. We make our way to the bar, among Aymeric's students and club regulars. Among these Laumière stalwarts is Jean, an instructor who sometimes stands in for Big Boss, but with a benevolence totally foreign to the head *coach*. To characterize Jean, I'd say two things. Firstly, in style, he's fearsomely handsome. Brown-haired, with two little blue beads in his eye sockets, muscular and impeccably coiffed, he's the spitting image of the ideal son-in-law. On the other hand, rumor has it that he's a spy. Jean is said to be a spy. That's why he's only present intermittently, as and when his missions require. I don't think that's what a secret agent looks like. To tell you the truth, I have no idea what a secret agent looks like "in real life". To be honest, I don't really care what Jean is up to after he's turned his back. Nevertheless, I have to admit that a legend like that, with a physique like that, is quite a man!

In the hubbub of the moment, the so-called spy compliments me, true to his habit of encouraging students rather than debunking them to titillate their pride. He judges that I "did pretty damn well" during my assault on Aymeric. I want to believe that's not just talk, although I'm still reeling from the spanking I've just taken. As I try to contain my dismay and focus on the moment, orders for pints of Grimbergen rain down like Gravelotte... until Aymeric explodes upon hearing my choice.

- A Coke, poor Nora?" he asks, aghast. Did you order a Coke?

I nod.

Even today, I remember the scene in minute detail. Of my hand clenching in my pocket, clutching my remaining fortune - four francs. Of my relief when I saw the price of Coke on the slate - four francs. Of my unease at the thought that, as a result, I won't be eating tonight, unless I manage to find something old at the bottom of a drawer.

So I can confirm that it will be a Coca for me. Aymeric's voice clicks. With his Parisian accent, he sounds like Arletty in Jean-Claude Van Damme's body:

- You're crazy, baby! Come on, I'll buy you a beer and we won't talk about it anymore. Deal?

I don't protest. I can't protest. Something crazy has just happened. Aymeric, the incredible Aymeric himself, the Aymeric who spends his classes - it seems to me - debunking me, this

Aymeric smiles at me, as if he's understood some of my confusion and unease. I have the impression that, beneath his mocking airs, he has enough empathy to read my mind. He doesn't know what I'm going through, no, he does: he feels it. So his smile, the first since I met Aymeric, I savor, I inhale, I ingest, and I guess it will stay with me for a long time. I may not be a killer in the ring yet, but who cares? I understand instantly that, at least for this smile, I was right to persevere in this sport.

As I savor this fleeting *flash*, the trainer rectifies my order, puts on his usual face and turns to the others, eyes to the sky.

- A Coke!" he murmurs. Tell me I'm dreaming...

As soon as the waiter returns with his full tray, the *coach* grabs a pint and exclaims:

- I raise my glass to Nora, who has finally deigned to come and have a drink with us! All I had to do was beat her up a little and she'd know who was boss...

The laughter of our table greets this joke, which is both innocent and nerve-wracking. I don't like overconfident guys, and yet the trainer's smile still warms me up inside.

When Aymeric asks me what I do for a living, I know in advance the reactions my answer will provoke, but I don't back down:

- I'm a philosophy student.

The guys who've heard it are waiting to see if they should laugh or act surprised. The *coach* decides for them.

- Like guys in togas who spend all their time in sandals asking themselves unanswerable questions? he quips.

- Nah, like a girl in *jeans* and tennis shoes asking herself essential questions. And not just essential questions, either. For example, what do you do?

Aymeric abruptly puts his hand in front of his mouth, shaking his head:

- I'm sorry, my dancer. I'm not going to tell you anything. If I do, I'll have to kill you afterwards, and with a pretty girl like you, that would be a shame... I can give you a hint, though: I always carry a Glock.

- A *what*?

Aymeric straightens slightly and lifts up his aviator jacket. A gun appears in part.

- Holy cow! Are you a bodyguard?

- Missed. Guys, don't tell him!

- So you're a cop.

- Bingo!

An icy chill shakes me. So this is a keuf in real life!

- Where do you work?

- I'm a captain with the Judicial Police in Paris. I'm with the BRI.

Chafouine the moment before, I'm suddenly dazzled. In my mind, the Brigade de Recherche et d'Intervention is made up of supermen who catch the biggest thugs and the worst terrorists. As someone who needs to admire a guy to get interested, I'm both served and embarrassed. Served, because the legend of the BRI makes me dream; and embarrassed because... well, up until now, I've cursed cops with a telluric rage.

In 1986, when I saw the images of the SAMU massaging and then taking the unfortunate Malik Oussekine to hospital, I remember my father watching TV like a madman, my mother crying and dragging me along in the flood of tears. In 1993, the murder of Makomé M'Bowolé in a police station in the eighteenth arrondissement and, in 1995, Mathieu Kassovitz's *La Haine, inspired by* this tragedy, rightly shook me and strengthened my conviction. I'm certain that a cop is a guy who's too stupid to do anything else. My father's account - so respectful of order since his arrival in France - of the corruption of Tunisian civil servants at the time didn't qualify my opinion. I'm convinced that "a cop obeys orders and disobeys the law".

Yes, as a philosopher, I like to ask myself questions; however, as human as any of us, I sometimes succumb to the siren song of clichés. I know all too well that prefabricated representations, vindictive beliefs and clear-cut judgments are reassuring and help to avoid "getting into one's head". And even people who aspire to think by deconstructing presuppositions, who study for it and fight with it to achieve it, even they sometimes fail to live up to their ambitions...

Luckily, that evening, Aymeric picked me up a second time after our assault. So, my question of the moment is: what if, after all, a cop isn't just a stupid bastard? What if a cop is also the guy who trains neighborhood kids as a volunteer two nights a week? I'm touched by the fact that a rookie is able to get involved in this club where mostly youngsters who are a bit lost are enrolled. For him, I imagine it's a way of getting a better idea of what's going on in our heads; and for us, he gives us - reluctantly - a more complex picture of his job.

As time went by, I discovered that many of the Laumière club's supervisors were police officers. You have to get to know each other to find out. It's not immediately obvious. How logical! Many young people would flee a club with condemned coaches. It takes time to build up a feeling of familiarity which, through habit,

The Philosopher of Barbès

turns into trust, masks come off and the confidences of the civil servants about some of the cases they've had to deal with reveal a much more engaging side to their job... and to them. We, the kids from the neighborhoods, discover with unabashed amazement that the cops have other activities than controlling young people or killing innocent people according to their faces. They have an essential role to play in ensuring our peace of mind; and some of them, like the BRI, risk their lives on our behalf every day.

I must admit that the BRI in particular fascinates me. In my imagination (and not only in mine), the face-to-face meeting on September 28, 1973 between Jacques Mesrine and Commissaire Robert Broussard is mythical. As a result, Aymeric skips the "Pinot simple cop" box and goes straight to the bright side of my fantasies: the real man, with a body and mind of steel, unshakeable honor and righteousness, who puts himself in danger to stop the real crooks. The Mennen man in hypermieux.

This epinal imagery echoes my childhood culture. Indeed, my image of the police is primarily televisual. I grew up with television. My parents didn't have any books. Or rather, there was only one book, renewed every week: *Télé 7 jours*. The other books that make their way into our apartment are smuggled in by a neighbor. In fact, this woman played a dual role in building me up. Firstly, by opening me up to stories that TV didn't tell; and secondly, by showing me that a right-wing, Chiracian woman is no more reducible to the clichés of a Mme Le Quesnoy than a cop is reducible to the antics of Gérard Jugnot.

When I was in elementary school, my neighbor gave me math lessons; when I went to secondary school, she gave me newspapers and books; above all, over the years, she has cared about me. This gift is priceless... even if it sometimes takes the form of money! On the day of my baccalaureate, this lady was the only one to know that I had obtained my diploma; she saluted my achievement with a five-hundred-franc bill. Afterwards, she was the only one who encouraged me to continue my studies. I owe her a lot, and I'm happy to write this book to express my infinite gratitude to her once again.

However, if I've stayed the course despite the exclusive omnipresence of TV, it's not solely responsible. My father's tastes helped me to avoid sinking into the most crass cretinism... and let's face it, reality TV didn't exist yet! Would this type of mind-numbing show have changed me? I would hope not, but I remain modest. Luckily, my father only watched three types of program:

- political broadcasts,
- action films like *Rocky* or *Rambo*, and
- detective series, from *Starsky and Hutch* to *Derrick*.

When he was on a building site, I was also allowed to watch cartoons, phew! The rest of the time, until I was in college and therefore freer to choose my books and go to the library, it was police and politics all the time. *In hindsight, I*'m forced to admit that TV does indeed shape us from childhood... but I'm immodest enough to hope that cases like mine also suggest that, whatever the pure spirits vomiting the small screen and its modern competitors, it's not always a catastrophe.

4.

It's obvious: I have to earn money. So I work and build my typical day around this obligation.

At seven o'clock, my alarm goes off. I wake up in my little room with no fridge or washing machine. When I get the chance, I gobble down whatever's lying around: a little canned soup, bread in a packet or, in the ultimate luxury, instant pasta. Then I head off to the Sorbonne - it's a good trot from home. At lunchtime, I work as a waitress. In the afternoon, I go back to work. At 5 p.m., I collect Léon from school until his parents arrive. Exceptional days are those when I add boxing or a psychoanalysis session to my dull schedule.

With what I earn as a waitress in hospital cafeterias in Paris, I have enough to survive, not enough to live on. Above all, at the hospital I discovered a logic that I knew in theory but was unaware of in practice: the hierarchy of social classes. Until recently, I hadn't left my neighborhood much... both geographically and in human terms. Once I'd left my parents' house, reading Marx or Bourdieu and frequenting the Jeunesses Communistes opened my eyes a little to what's at stake in the relationship with capital. Today, I can see that the little waitress that I am is getting along just fine.

- with nurses, stretcher-bearers, orderlies and cleaners;

- pretty well with externals and internals;

- moderately well with attending physicians; and

- terrible with medical professors, especially the older specimens of this caste.

The pundits I meet, incredibly full of themselves, drunk with the syrupy deference in which they seem to bathe, see in me nothing but a bit of fresh flesh. Clearly, their only goals when they become aware of my existence are to demand to be served in a second, and to see if there's any way they can get the little Arab girl to sleep with them. My looks must seem exotic to them. It's an understatement to say that their unhealthy authoritarianism, insistent glances and libidinous allusions disgust me.

Looking back, I think I admire my patience. I don't know if I'd be able to contain myself today in the face of those caricatures. More than once, I've swallowed the gestures and words that angered me. Their insulting disdain - and not just for me, far from it - made me want to grab them by the collar and spit in their faces the tirade of the hospital's little hand:

- You're no better than me, understand? You're a professor of medicine, *cool*. So what if I am? You got fancy degrees? Good for you. You're loaded? Good for you. Surrounded by flatterers? If that's your thing... And, sometimes, you save lives? Respect, but that doesn't give you the right to crush others. Quite the opposite, in fact. Given your profession, given your rank, you should be the example of benevolence. Except that you have such a huge *ego* that you think you're entitled to step on everyone around you. That's why, in my eyes, you'll never be the genius or legend you imagine yourself to be.

I must add a nuance to these vituperations, because the attitude of the pundits has a collateral effect: it brings us closer together. "We", that is, those who are considered less than nothing by the lords of the hospital. That's a lot of people, from stretcher-bearers to nurses and medical secretaries! There are often just a few of us left when our shifts are over. This allows me to meet extraordinary people in every hospital I work in. At Cochin, Bichat and Beaujon, the same class dichotomy is implacable, arousing the same anger. When I find myself in this state of nerves in front of a lord of the AP-HP, I have the renewed certainty that I was right to find an outlet for my anger in boxing.

On a daily basis, I have to draw on my unsuspected reserves to keep going. Psychologically, so as not to get carried away, and physically too. At the end of each shift, I have to clean the cafeteria floor with bleach. The problem is that the soles of my shoes have holes in them. So the bleach soaks my socks. The first day, it's not pleasant, but nothing serious. By the end of the week, this daily bath is burning my skin and making me suffer. Even though I'm not very choosy, I end up buying Nivea cream to cope! This suffering is all the more acute because it reminds me of my precarious situation, so far removed from the one I could have dreamed of in my twenties. I think my mother cleaned houses and I do too... except that I don't even have proper soles. On days when I'm feeling down, it makes me feel as if I've started from a low point and yet managed to fall. I have the distinct feeling that I've hit rock bottom and am still sinking.

My parents came from the boondocks, facing appalling dangers and conditions. My father, singularly, came in the hold of a ship with maybe fifty francs in his pocket. He managed to disembark in Marseille and find his brother in Paris, which was quite a feat. And now I'm burning my feet scrubbing the floor in front of people who look down on me. I feel like I've missed everything. That I've betrayed my family once again, having let them down by giving up on a golden marriage whose benefits would have trickled down to them. What if my philosophy studies were just a smokescreen that was finally dissipating, letting me see the reality of my condition?

In short, I'm in low spirits. There's only one thing keeping my head above water: I'm going to make it. I've got this hope ingrained in me. When the spirit fails, my animal instincts take over. Adversity is nothing but a test. It's up to me to stay the course. My shrink tells me I have an extraordinary capacity for resilience. At the time, these words sounded hollow to me. What sounded solid was my visceral conviction that I'd get through it.

More than once, *Scarface* has saved me. In Tony Montana, I, who never in the least aspired to become the first drug dealer in the history of mankind (nor the last, for that matter!), draw my strength. In her trajectory, I read my life path. In her journey, I find details of my life:

- the obligation to work in rotten bars;

- physical pain; and

- the feeling of humiliation, all the more keenly felt because it undermines confidence in the future and in oneself.

Among my heroes, I also cling to the figure of my father. Even though I know the faults of the man who made his wife my mother, his example stays with me. He's the inaccessible star that guides me on clear or overcast days. Did he become violently imperfect? Yes, but he fought harder than I did. To settle in Paris. To work on building sites, getting up early and enduring racist insults from his bosses and even his colleagues. To bequeath to my brother Malik and me the few cards he was able to amass before we tackled life's poker table. If he has accumulated these micro-miracles in the face of gigantic difficulties, I *must be* able to do it in spite of my minor worries.

Better still, thanks to them. Whatever happens, I'll find a solution. My only task is to find the energy to do it. A maximum or a minimum of energy, depending on the moment. But always the energy not to give up. Not to submit to traditions that don't suit me. Not to hang around the neighborhood waiting for things to happen. Not to give in to degrading propositions. In short, to live with my head held high, whatever the cost.

Besides, as much as it pains me to struggle so much - and I do, of course I do! - I'm not the one who's worried. The tragedy of my life is to feel that my brother doesn't have this sacred fire within him. Why doesn't he believe in himself, when we have the same hero-who's-going-out references in our noggins? What's he lacking to have that *blast*, that violent intuition that, come on, you've got to go for it, exist on your own and build yourself up, and never mind if it's a bit bumpy, if it's rocky, if it challenges the harmful comfort of the habits that undermine us?

That's another reason why I'm writing this book. It's not to give an exemplary and admirable "life lesson", but to encourage all readers who are fighting, sometimes against themselves, to move forward with dignity towards their own self-fulfilment... and to boost the morale of readers who are no longer fighting because they've let themselves be persuaded by deterministic arguments ("you're not from the right neighborhood, you didn't follow the right path, you're poor, etc.") that they're good for nothing.

Everyone is who they are. I'm not a role model. On the other hand, I'm willing, in my own way, to be the Tony Montana of readers who recognize themselves in the description I've just sketched! With one difference: I don't know what I want to be, but I do know what I don't want to be. Religion, in its moral aspect, helps me. When you're hungry, very hungry - and not just for a few hours: every day, all the time, like a song that won't leave you, humming or howling according to the moment - and someone offers you the chance to earn hundreds of francs in a few hours by becoming an "*escort*" or "charm actress", according to hypocritical euphemisms, despite the specific nature of the work that would chill many, only a solid moral code can prevent you from giving in to temptation.

Mind you, I understand perfectly well why women are forced to accept these assignments. How can I criticize their decision? I simply explain that, in my case, my faith in God has protected me from this hypothesis. Stubbornly, I cling to my ethics and my will to succeed on my own by working in a profession I love, in which I can blossom and which, very prosaically, will feed me. Finally. I've gone too many days without eating to overlook this aspect. I have too many childhood memories, vivid as they are, of making sure we didn't "eat too much" on Mondays, in order to make it through to Thursday with the special of the day. I have so many such anecdotes in my mind that I'm not interested in wealth. I want to eat my fill, and therefore find a situation that my parents would have something to be proud of.

This eternal quest for parental pride is undoubtedly what frustrates a large part of the second generation of Arabs, to which I belong. We struggle to conquer our parents' pride, all the more so as, even when they are proud of us, they struggle to verbalize it. On a personal level, aware of the infinite nature of this quest, I'm learning to create substitutes for myself. For example, while I'm waiting for my parents to be proud of me, I try to make my shrink and my boxing coach proud of me. With them, and in the hope that my parents will one day congratulate me, I concentrate my efforts on a single goal: to get out of my condition as a poor girl with no future.

The struggle is fierce. It's at this strategic moment that fate decides to add another layer and deliver a heavy blow to the Lakheal family.

5.

That afternoon, telephone. I don't feel like answering. The answering machine goes off and lets me hear the message:

- Nora, it's your mother. Please call again. Your father is...

I throw myself on the handset and shout:

- What?

- Ah, Nora... Your poor father is at his worst.

- What's wrong with it?

- He'd rather be dead.

- What the hell is wrong with him?

- Your brother has been shot in the shoulder. He's in custody at the Louis Blanc police station. Go and look after him, darling. Your father is as unhappy as a rock.

- I'm on my way.

I wouldn't go straight to the police station without checking the information. In true Tunisian fashion, my mother is a *drama queen*. I want to find out for sure before I venture into a police station. And then, I confess, it's also an opportunity to see my parents again. Two years without seeing each other was getting a bit old.

When I arrive, my father is lying on the sofa, a wet towel on his forehead. In the code of the older generation of Arabs, this means, "I'm at the end of my life." He speaks to me in a barely audible faint, almost grumbling voice.

- My daughter... Your brother is a loser... A nobody... Doing this to us...

- What did he do to you?

- He disgraced us... He killed his poor father on his birthday...

I'm trying to reconstruct the events. Apparently, under the combined effect of the disinhibiting *shit*, the exciting Subutex and the pack of little assholes he hangs out with, my brother has turned his head upside down. Tipping over into hyperviolence, he and his buddies ransacked three stores on rue du Faubourg-Saint-Denis, exciting the pit bulls recruited for the occasion... until a Turkish retoucher revolted and fired into the crowd with his self-defense pistol. My brother took charge. The police arrived. They took the wounded man to Lariboisière hospital and then took him into custody. End of story, beginning of drama.

Because my father, the tough guy who used to box Tunisian cops, has a visceral fear of the French police. His motto since he's been in France: don't rock the boat. The country has welcomed us, so we have to take it easy. It's basic prudence. For my father, justice is like medicine: you know when you start with them, never when you're rid of them. In other words, in his behavior, there's both an act and a real distrust of the justice system in his new country. Behind the expressionistic excess of the man lying with a towel over his face, I see my father, that rock, shaken.

I can't believe it. As much as I was ready for a pure sketch, I feel that, behind the *drama king*, there *is* a wounded and worried man. Perhaps even, through his character as a dying man, he, the unyielding colossus, is admitting that his son's police custody is intimately overwhelming him. Especially as he imagines that police custody is like his own experience in Tunisia, where it lasts a fortnight, with no right to a lawyer or doctor. And here, his hero, his successor, his first wonder of the world, he can't protect him. His powerlessness must be adding fuel to the fire of his dismay.

I try to reassure him as much as possible by saying:

- Okay, calm down, I'm going to Louis Blanc. I'll take care of it.

My mother walks me to the door and whispers:

- After that, you know, if you want to come back and live with us...

- We'll see," I growl to cut it short.

I leave my family's apartment ultra-serviced. I realize that, in the two years since I left, no one here has changed. It feels like a terrible waste. Given my brother's abilities, I think my parents have missed the boat. Malik is smart. Cute. Polite. Sporty. Full of promise. But, to his misfortune, he's also the little male of the household, the great prince, the future of the family; and this status is crushing him as slowly as it is surely crushing him. My mother tried too hard to please my brother, anticipating his desires the better to fulfill them. My father showed him off like a trophy. Malik was their pride and joy, whatever he did or didn't do.

As a result, he stopped working at school: why bother? In seventh grade, he was directed towards a technological stream with a mechanical option - what we call a dead end, in the truest sense of the word! The idea might seem laudable. Except that this sidetrack brings together those left behind by the French education system, those who couldn't fit into the general stream - and not those who would be thrilled at the idea of learning a trade in a field they're passionate about. And yet, pretending to teach mechanics to rebellious kids who don't give a damn: what a waste of time! what distress for teachers, especially when lack of resources accentuates their demotivation! and, for the kids, what a catastrophe!

Malik smokes his first joint in his new establishment. It was there that he discovered the scum code. It's where he builds himself a counter-model which, without him even realizing it, distances him from both society and his own self-fulfillment. Concerned about his evolution, I fought. On the day he was taken into custody, I had to admit defeat. My parents' lack of lucidity, the resignation of the French education system and my brother's poor choices led him to the cell that afternoon, with lead pellets in his shoulder. I was powerless to prevent it.

Stunned, I set off on foot for the police station. On the way, between anger and worry, I perceive only snatches of my surroundings. Shadows. Flecks of color. Movement. From a store comes the *flow of* Maxi Jazz, as if speaking directly to me.

> *I used to worry. Thought I was going mad in a hurry. Getting stressed, making excessive mess in darkness. No electricity.*
> *Something's all over me, greasy.*
> *Insomnia, please, release me!*[1]

In a daze, I arrive at my destination. On learning of the purpose of my visit, the surly policewoman on duty gives me a scornful pout and points me in the direction of the station chief, the spitting image of Achille Talon:

---

1. "I was worried / I felt like I was going up the towers at full speed / I was stressed, it was messy in the dark / No electricity… I was assaulted by a sticky thing that oppressed me / Steuplaît, Insomnie, lâche-moi!" (Faithless, "Insomnia")

- You see with him.

The guy doesn't say: "And now, without any extra charge, hop, our table of contents", like the character with the big nose. Just, in a good-natured tone:

- Is your brother in custody? What a good idea! It must keep you busy when you're in trouble... And what's this hero's name?

- Malik Lakheal.

- Ha, is that your brother, the little idiot who took a beating? You'll have to do something for him, won't you, Miss? Otherwise, things are going to get ugly...

I quite agree with the diagnosis, but I didn't come to debate education and family life with a stranger. Just as I'm about to refocus our exchange, two policemen arrive with a young black man in handcuffs. The guy is overexcited and insults the police copiously.

- Achilles grunts. Cage him next to the other gibbon and we'll deal with him when he calms down.

The other "gibbon"? Sorbonne student that I am, I don't know the term. No time to ask for a subtitle. Only later will I discover the meaning of this insult. Already, the big-nosed racist went on:

- As for you, mademoiselle, you look devastated, so I'm going to do you a favor. I'm going to let you see your brother through the glass. That's all I can do. I shouldn't have to, but since I'm the boss...

He turns to an agent and shouts:

- Vivien," Malik shows his sister.

- Who's Malik?

- The injured man.

The next thing I know, my brother is *groggy*. On his right side, his arm and shoulder are hidden by a huge bandage. The proud arm I know doesn't give a damn. I hear him murmur:

The Philosopher of Barbès

- Sorry...

I don't know what to say to him. It's neither an ordinary attitude for him, nor a banal word in his mouth. So, in a small voice, I express for the first and last time one of the intangible truths that guide my life:

- Malik, I love you.

I'd never imagined I'd ever say it. But in the spontaneity of emotion, I let my heart speak. Immediately, I see the big man behind the glass transform into my little brother. His eyes mist up. He bows his head and breathes:

- Fuck, I screwed up...

- It's going to be okay.

- Nah, I really messed up...

- Are you listening to me, Malik? I'm telling you it's going to be okay.

- On Dad's birthday, of all days... How could I?

Again, words fail me to comfort him. I can only find a few banalities to slip in:

- What's done is done. Now it's time to get out. We're here for you. Dad, mom and me. Don't forget it. Do you promise?

He raises his head. His eyes meet mine. They speak to me in silence, and I understand every nuance of their language. I try to crack a smile, then turn away, my jaws clenched. There's only one thing on my mind now: not to cry in the police station. The Lakheals don't cry. We're strong. I have to be, too. How would I look, in tears, in front of these strangers in uniform? I want to get out into the street as soon as possible.

Seeing me reappear, Achille Talon tells me that, brof, my brother will be taken to the Palais de Justice in Paris the next day. I manage to slip in:

- Thank you, sir, we'll be there.

Then I'm off to Kremlin-Bicêtre.

I don't want to go back to my parents. At least not right now. I'll just give them a quick report by phone and tell them about the next morning's court appearance. We'll talk about the rest later. Because as soon as I saw Malik in his cell, I *knew* I had to accept my mother's offer to move back in with them. It's about time.

I've got to come back and straighten out this family that's going to hell in a handbasket. No one else can do it. Only I can and must prevent my brother from falling into a spiral that could lead him to commit far more serious acts - a robbery, why not? In a way, through the voice of Achille Talon, saving Malik is the first preventive mission entrusted to me by the police!

6.

It was at the Palais de Justice in Paris that I finally understood what I was going to do with my life.

To everyone, especially to the kids who are a little lost, crushed by their wearisome living conditions and damaged by the generalized defeatism that ensues, I hope one day to experience this apocalypse in the Greek sense of ἀποκάλυψις, *apokálupsis*, which designates the revelation of a hitherto veiled truth. Sometimes, the apocalypse seems to appear out of nowhere. In reality, it resolves the equation with its many unknowns, where our experiences, our heartbreaks, our disappointed and enduring hopes, our suspended questions, our worries and our personalities all lapping at the surface.

In my case, however incongruous it may seem, I discovered the meaning of my life on my way to my brother's court appearance. Time has erased some of the details of that half-day. Yet the *flashes* that remain are exceptionally vivid. There are five of them.

ACT I: APPEARANCE

At first glance, I remember what time it is when I see my father's silhouette. In the distance, at the end of a long corridor. It's 10:25.

He, who in some aspects of his life is not a symbol of immaculate perfection, stands straight, dignified, silent. I don't know what's going on in his head. In mine, it's obviously clearer.

I think of the twenty-five years he spent in France. The dreams he must have had. The disappointments he endured and sometimes made others endure. To his dismay at seeing his son questioned. To his twenty-five years of jackhammering, impossible hours and customary contempt. To the courage of all his fellow chibanis. And to his dignity, at this very moment.

My lyrical flights of fancy are shattered in mid-air when my mother, catching sight of me, resumes her *drama queen* role. Here's the second highlight of the morning.

ACT II: THE ACTRESS

- My fiiiiiiils!" moaned my mother, crying loudly. My poor fiiiiiils!

Embarrassed by this spectacle, I hurry to join her and tell her to stop this bad joke as soon as possible. I feel like a stranger to what's going on. I've activated my usual defense mechanism: if I want to help my family, I have to be both physically close to them and mentally outside their mess. I'm here and elsewhere. Involved and detached. At stake: my survival. Identifying myself is out of the question. Too risky.

Especially as, that morning, my mother was furious with me. The day before, she'd suggested I come back into the family fold. Now she's blaming me for everything. In twelve hours, I've become a nobody. I'm the one who didn't fight for my brother;

I'm the one who, without reacting, let him get bogged down in his difficulties at school. So Malik's arrest? My fault, think.

- Since you left, everything's gone to pot! Oh, you must feel good! I'm so glad you got rid of us! For leaving us with our problems! You see the result? My poor fiiiiiiiiiiils!

- Come on, you can stop now. I'm not responsible for anything. You're the one who kicked me out. And I don't think this is the right place or the right time to talk.

My mother turns to my father for support. One look from Ahmed is enough to make him swallow his chewing gum. Perhaps, like me, in this moment of anxiety, he's tired of this endless comedy. I am, anyway. I'm trying to get past it, but I am. Even if being reunited with your family after two years apart is an immeasurable joy, going - overnight - from the status of savior to the rank of last of the ungrateful ones doesn't make anyone happy. No one ever is. Hot and cold, the CAC 40 mindset of always checking whether my share price is rising or falling, very little for me. I'm simply disappointed that my mother doesn't have the honesty to recognize that, between us, if anyone's to blame, it's not so much the accused as the accuser.

And then came the third scene, which I now remember in its entirety.

ACT III: THE DEAF

As we stand in the middle of the room, three policemen, no doubt emerging from the depot where they'd left their prisoner in a cell, walk past us. True to form, my father greets them with an audible:

- Good afternoon, gentlemen.

No response. The guys pass by without calculating. My father is invisible. Because he's dressed like an old chibani? I think so. Why else would he be subjected to this degrading silence? I whisper to my dad:

- Don't worry, they must have been thinking about something else, they didn't hear you.

- Probably, girl. So, it doesn't matter, you know. It doesn't matter...

Anger overwhelms me. Yes, it's serious.

I look at the three cops walking away with a rage I didn't know I had. I want to scream: "Hey, you morons! My father is worth ten of you! Aren't you idiots ashamed of your contempt? You represent France and all French people, even those you deem different from you, you bastards!" No need to shout. I suspect that hearing would go to the civil servants... and that would call into question the pseudo-deafness of these racists, the fragile and last bulwark that preserves my father's honor.

I understand my father all the more because I experience the same ambivalence as he does. I'd rather move forward despite difficulties and betrayals than feel sorry for myself. If I take the negative side of my story, I'll see myself as a victim of the conditions in which I was raised. I'd much rather stand up and say to myself: "It's true, Nora, your parents were no cakewalk, but you can raise yourself and help them at the same time." From my father, I prefer to remember

- political awareness,

- respect for the state,

- a sense of loyalty and

- the courage to go to work, even if it means getting up at four in the morning to suffer and be scorned.

Allowing yourself to be inspired by imperfect people is a good way of growing yourself and striving to love these humans despite their shortcomings.

ACT IV: LIBERATION

As I continue to rant, my brother's court-appointed lawyer appears and announces:

- Given that this is his first offence, that he is a minor and that he presents the required guarantees of representation, he will be released.

My mother takes the court officer's hands and kisses them with an effusion that is both sincere and overplayed - a paradoxical specialty mastered by Tunisian mothers.

- Thank you, Madame, thank you...

My father insists:

- Are you sure? Are you done?

- Your son will be released soon. Not in a minute! It takes time for the papers to be completed, signed and stamped, and for your son to collect his belongings; but, in the next few hours, I guarantee you'll be able to hug him and take him home. On the other hand...

I see my father stiffen.

- ... Mr. Ferhat is going to ask you for compensation for the ransacking of his store," concludes the lawyer.

- We'll pay whatever it takes," says my father. He can count on us.

Reassured for the apple of their eye, my parents take me back to the Cité metro station. I don't want to stay any longer. For today, my task is done. I've had enough. I'm tired. Completely out of shape. A little depressed. Only one sentence in my head: get off my back. Give me some air. Out!

ACT V: THE REVELATION

I descend the subway stairs. My parents are walking away. And suddenly, light comes to me. An absolute certainty - rare for a philosopher! - seized me. I'm going to take the competitive exam to become a police officer.

How could I not have thought of this before? Yesterday's scene at the police station and today's, when the officers snubbed my father, convinced me... but Immanuel Kant had prepared the ground by laying down, in the first part of the *Metaphysics of Morals*, in 1785, the keystone of his categorical imperative: "Act in such a way that you treat humanity, both in your own person and in every other person, always at the same time as an end, and never merely as a means." I don't know if I'm the first sick person to want to become a Condé because of an eighteenth-century German philosopher, but I'll take it!

I want an end to police racism. I want to speak out against injustice. Against the inequalities in treatment that I find intolerable. Against the misuse of republican law, both by the police and by delinquents. Nothing new: I'm the sum of the "no's" I've said and that guide my life. No to an arranged marriage. No to the fate of an uneducated, submissive woman. No to those who saw my father as a tick who had come to suck and corrupt the blood of France. In the face of all these no's, *yes,* I'm going to be useful. Not to live and dream as Julien Clerc sang. Just useful to live. With and by others as much as by myself.

As a single woman, the philosopher, the Muslim, the boxer and the Tunisian-born woman in me will take the competitive examination to become a police officer and serve the people and the nation of France. I, Nora, am going to pacify relations between citizens and police, and between police and citizens. Don't worry: right away, I'm sure I've just described a fantasy. What does it matter, as long as this dream gives me the strength to face up to a challenge and do what I can, just as I'm trying to do for my family? I won't save the world, any more than I saved Malik, but I'll have gone as far as I can. And if I can't get the lines of injustice to move, I want to give it a try. To contribute. I don't want to limit myself to the easy role of the critic. To be an actress, even if it means playing a second or hundredth role.

In short, piece by piece, the *puzzle* comes together. The boxing teacher, agent of the BRI. My brother's misdeeds, punished by racist cops. My father's contempt for the police at the Palais de Justice. My doubts. My desire for justice. And I deduce that my philosophy studies are leading me to the opposite of philosophy: the police.

I never say to myself that I'm giving up on a prestigious or pompous diploma. On the contrary, I'm convinced that this is the culmination of my quest. Thanks to psychoanalysis, philosophy and a mixture of narcotics absorbed by my brother's gang, I've found my way. In the police force, I'm going to be useful immediately. It's through the police that people's lives pass, when difficulties arise. The police are where I want to be. That I'm going to be.

All I have to do is pass a competition, then I can save humanity. That's all there is to it!

7.

The peacekeeper's exam is in three months. To kick off the sprint symbolically, I start by resigning from university. In other words, I'm saying goodbye to Jean Maurel, the John Keating - played by Robin Williams in *The Dead Poets Society* - of the university where I study. It's important to me. His class starts at 8:30 but, on this day as every week, his disciples have been outside the door for three quarters of an hour. The infatuation with this teacher is justified: he transports his students, including me. Always quick with a good word, he transforms his podium into a stage, capturing attention with his atypical and effective teaching methods.

On a personal level, he propelled me into the art world. When I arrived in his lecture hall, this universe stopped for me at the borders of *The A-Team*. I'm not exaggerating. Ever since I discovered this oddball, I've been looking forward to his weekly artistic bread. Today, I'm a little afraid. I want to tell the Great Guru how much he's changed my life and, in the process, tell him of my decision. How could he, an inveterate anarchist, not be offended to learn that I'm leaving his course to prepare to become a bastard cop?

For a long time this week, I've been lying awake thinking about how I'd justify such an affront to him. Even if you can't teach an old tiger to quiver its whiskers, I thought of arguing that, without security (and therefore without police), there can be no equality, and no livable society for those who love wisdom. Then the opposition between Hegel and Hobbes came to mind. That's good, for a philosophy teacher... and it seems more than appropriate!

Indeed, Hobbes believes that a strong state is preferable to anarchy, because "man is a wolf to man". It has to be said that he was writing after a very violent civil war. He therefore argued that the rule of law could only exist if the police ensured a form of harmony. Hegel, on the other hand, believed in the continuous evolution of mankind over the centuries. His idealism leads him to imagine that the world will soon be perfect, as History leads humanity towards its completion. So, if philosophy were as binary as a boxing match, I'd be more Hobbesian than Hegelian... just as I'm more Ali than Foreman!

I won't get a chance to say my piece. No sooner had I stammered out my admiration and decision, Jean Maurel nearly fainted. You have to imagine this big-bearded head as a cross between Victor Hugo (of whom he's a specialist) and François Corbier (singer and host of Club Dorothée, of which he probably knows nothing), who opens his mouth wide as if he were suffocating and gasping for air. The man puts his right hand to his throat, takes a deep breath and, staggering, starts walking towards the window, terrified:

- How dare you contemplate a crime of this nature? What you're teaching me is appalling! How dreadful! What can I say? The world is coming to an end! I don't want to believe it. I-don't-want-to-believe-it.

At the end of his journey, he raises his eyes to the sky and stays there for a moment. I remember this image better than if

The Philosopher of Barbès

I'd photographed it. The large, slightly peeling wooden door. The color of the light filtered by the dust on the glass. His outfit, too: grey pants, burgundy shirt, blue tie. Suddenly, caught in his trance, the professor starts mumbling as if to himself:

- What on earth did I say to give her such an idea?

With vague eyes, he calls out to me:

- Help me, you! What harm have I done to deserve that one of my flock should come and stab me in the heart, and thank me to boot? If she chose the worst direction in the world after enjoying my course, what path would she have taken if my course had displeased her?

He seems to come out of his dream and, staring at me, very serious, insists:

- I'm asking you.

I press my lips together. I know his provocation doesn't call for a response. Especially not a debate between Hobbes and Hegel. Suddenly, a smile lights up this character's face. The comedy is over. I hesitate to applaud this unconventional reaction, but, grabbing his coat, the man anticipates and exits, majestic, saying:

- Have a nice trip, miss!

It's not exactly how I'd anticipated the skit, but I'm still in a daze. Clinging to the desk, I realize that I've just spoken to my favorite teacher for the first and last time. There's no turning back now: my student life is over.

For the last time too, I take the staircase to the courtyard. I try to take in the beauty of this baroque architecture and the magic that emanates from it, even as I move through it on a daily basis. All around me, preoccupied or carefree, the students bustle about, hail each other or continue on their way, immersed in their thoughts. After Hobbes and Hegel, the question of another philosopher of a peculiar kind - Patrick Bruel, to name but one - crosses my mind as I wonder what my former classmates will be like in twenty years' time. I don't yet know that, among my more or less close college acquaintances, one will become a philosopher and a very active campaigner against violence and racism in the police force, which she describes as being, today as in the past, the armed arm of the State's totalitarian and colonial ideology. It's amazing how, by taking more or less the same courses, you can become a cop or an anti-cop!

Today, with a few rare exceptions, I keep very few friends from those days. The philosophy curriculum brought together people who were socially too different from me. You can love diversity and still find it hard to get on the same wavelength as your class-mate. When you spend all your time, hungry, chasing money, it's hard to vibrate at the same frequency as the person who lives in an apartment a stone's throw from the university and has no other plan than to go to class and study, either to become *the* new philosopher, or to branch off into theology, the specialty favored by the traditionalist Catholics around me.

I have no complaints about "the privileges of the privileged", despite my sporadic annoyance at the arrogance and even arrogance they sometimes exude. I'm not even jealous of the material conditions in which they study. In the hushed atmosphere of philosophy classes, there's no class struggle: a wall of incommunicability takes its place. Too tired by my struggle to survive and help my family, too cautious perhaps, I didn't know how to crack it, or didn't dare. Afraid, perhaps, that others might *also* inflate me in the process. Life is enough for me.

In fact, from my university studies, I've retained above all the visceral conviction that philosophy shouldn't be confined to the walls of the university. Contrary to what one might fear, there's nothing abstract or elucidatory about philosophizing. It's not a domain reserved for those who like to indulge in concepts worthy of the aporias of quantum physics, play the expert by quoting Heidegger in the text, or display their expertise on the vision of Husserlian phenomenology unfolded by Rudolf Bernet in *The Life of the Subject*. Philosophy is very concrete and very useful. It's all about thinking against yourself, against your convictions, against the obvious.

Yes, to philosophize is first and foremost to question our tendency to binarize the world. To put it more plainly, it's to posit that there isn't, on the one hand, what's right (i.e. what I think) and, on the other, what's wrong and therefore deserves to be ignored or, better still, destroyed. In my daily life, as far as I'm able, I like to listen to other people's thoughts in order to put mine to the test, to question it, to refine it and then modify it... or to confirm it when, after examination, my opinion doesn't seem all that stupid! Like the pre-Socratic philosophers, albeit with my own limits that I'm constantly trying to push back, I struggle to distrust truths set in stone. As my beloved Immanuel Kant reminds us, we all need a framework to move forward and orient ourselves in thought and in the world; in return, we must allow ourselves to be challenged by the discourse, reasoning and argumentation of others.

Practical proof? Preparing for the police exam while I'm a philosophy degree student may seem ridiculous and derisory. But I'm certain that, in my case, it doesn't mean wasting my life. It's not giving up on the prospect of a degree that would be all the more beautiful if earned by the daughter of a laborer and a cleaning lady. It doesn't mean giving up on the less controversial careers that such a diploma would have opened up, from journalist to teacher, for example. On the contrary, it means daring to go against the obvious and align my life plan with my convictions.

Isabelle, my psychoanalyst, understands this instantly and encourages me in this direction. Her words mean a lot to me, because she's been with me since the day a social studies teacher at Tolbiac, himself a shrink, said to me as an aside, after reading an assignment:

- Little one, listen to what I'm going to say before you tell me I'm interfering in something that's none of my business. You need to start therapy. You absolutely must. Otherwise, you'll be shooting yourself in no time.

Aware of the frailties I was trying to hide under my tough-as-nails shell, I called the number he'd given me. Despite my limited means, Isabelle agreed to see me. Since then, she's followed my progress in a demanding and benevolent way, and my police project seems to her to be consistent with what she knows about me. But that doesn't stop her from asking the burning question.

- Have you told your parents?" she asks.

- No, not yet. I'm waiting for the right moment.

- There'll never be a good time. Not with them. Act according to *your* agenda.

I nod and, on my way out, decide to go and tell my family about my project. Except that, as luck would have it, I take the metro in the wrong direction. A missed opportunity? Of course it was! All things considered, I'd rather miss my announcement than fail my competition.

8.

Three months later, 1997 is drawing to a close. I'm ready to face my new challenge.

I studied the reference book to prepare for the exam. I spent days and days revising the psycho-technical tests, those fascinating questionnaires where you learn to determine as quickly as possible whether the large square can contain the small circle and other nonsense supposed to check whether the candidate is disturbed... and whose results can be used during the eventual oral. I accumulated ten hours of sport a week. In addition to boxing at Laumière, I take advantage of the preparation offered by the Préfecture de Police on Wednesdays. I run; I work on high jumps and long jumps; I climb rope. At *weekends, I manage to* fit in another training session at Vincennes, with boxing in the morning and *jogging* in the woods in the afternoon. I've never been as muscular in my life as I was then! What's more, having returned to live with my parents, I managed to find a job. The aim: to have enough money to buy a suitcase and some clothes - especially sportswear - and to keep a few banknotes "just in case". I'm unstoppable, and I like it.

My determination paid off. The first round of the competition smiles on me. I was declared eligible. In the second round, I had to face a psychologist focused on an obsession:

- Do you think the police are racist, Miss?

You know, it's my fault, am I stupid? I have the face and name of an Arab. Racism is a good subject for "people like us". Calmly, I try to explain that I don't believe the institution itself is racist. If it were, would I want to join? On the other hand, as in all professions, the police force is bound to have a few morons who are entrenched in their racial prejudices.

- If you had to work with a colleague "steeped in prejudice", my examiner insists, how do you think you'd behave?

The shrink pisses me off. She probably does it on purpose, but she does it very well. Would she ask such questions of an evelyn-edurand? At the time, I don't see the need for such insistence. Later, I'll realize that it's probably the most pertinent question I've been asked during the entire competition. Indeed, my interlocutor *knows* that I'm going to come across a whole host of more or less unabashed racists if I join the institution. For the time being, barely masking my annoyance, I simply reply:

- Well, what do you want me to do? If he makes reprehensible remarks in my presence, I won't let them pass, respecting my position and the law.

And I add, mentally, "Now will you get off my back with your nutty questions?" Maybe "nuts" isn't the word I'm thinking of; never mind, I've forgotten the word that actually crossed my mind.

The psychologist seems satisfied with what I've said and with having tested my resistance to irritation. After this tense moment, we head for Pantin, where the sports tests await us in the middle of a housing estate. Some candidates let it be known that, every year, local "youths" come to disrupt the tests by throwing stones at the future cops. These rumors - we won't be attacked in the slightest - annoy me, because those who spread them are idiots complaining about being stigmatized as future police officers. Nevertheless, they are quick to stigmatize those who have done nothing to them. Who are the real aggressors in this case? This stupidity on the part of my perhaps future colleagues infuriates me. Chic, I can't think of a more effective stimulant! The proof is that I'm slamming home excellent results, including the best high jump of my session.

After this *climax* comes the hard part: waiting for the results. At least that's what I think. I'm having a hard time. Just as difficult is the way my friends look at me. At parties, even close girlfriends welcome me to the sound of "Sound of da police", the KRS-One hit that DJ Cut Killer remixed for *La Haine,* because "it's the sound of da police" seems to mean "police assassin". Adding gravy to this not-so-fresh kebab, the classic anti-cop jokes follow me around, as if I were now just "that" - a policewoman. Encouraged, the smart guys go on and on with pseudo *punchlines* like:

- Hey, Nora! Won't you smoke a spliff with us before entering your convent? It'd be so much fun to share a joint with a keuf!

Even though these jabs take their toll in the long run, I end up steeling myself against them. I don't hear them any more, and I can almost put them down to a sense of humor that's not really there.

On the other hand, some of my buddies disappoint me by taking my new direction badly. Neither positive nor joking, they simply cut me off. According to them, I've betrayed them. They oscillate between amazement and bitterness. They imagined I was going to become the opposite of a peace officer. They have arguments... or what they think are arguments. With them, I went to high school in Stalingrad, which - to put it mildly - was never the poshest neighborhood in Paris. With them, I hung out at Porte de la Chapelle. With them, I sang NTM, including the famous "Police":

The notion of humanism no longer exists when they put on the uniform (…),
Worse still if, in their manual, your color doesn't match (…).
How can you claim to be defending the State when you yourself are
intoxicated, often mentally retarded?

With them, I drank whey milk when Public Enemy slipped its anthem into our enthusiastic ears:

Fuck tha policeComin' straight from the underground,Young nigger got it bad cuz I'm brownAnd not the other color. So police thinkThey have the authority to kill a minority.[2]

So when I turn up and announce that I *want to* be a cop, that I've worked for it and that it looks pretty good, they must think I've fallen into the most detestable fascism. Like my little friends in the Pantin stadium, they who complain of being the victims of clichés are taking the same shortcuts of blind detestation… all the more dangerous for being so quick and simple. Why tell ourselves that, behind the "bougnoule" or the "keuf", there's often someone interesting to discover, when it's so simple and so unifying to

---

2. "Fuck the police / If I come out of my shithole, I'm in trouble because I'm just a little nigger / not the right color. That's why the cops think / they've got the right to kill me, since I'm a minority."

immediately disqualify a group of people bearing a stigma such as skin color or uniform?

After these disappointments, I'm not out of the woods yet. It may seem strange, but in February 1998, I opened the long-awaited letter containing the good news I'd been hoping for: I'd passed the competitive examination to become a peacekeeper. It was an earthquake for my family.

My parents are devastated. How could my father, who is certainly retired from cars but an ex-rebel imprisoned in Tunisia, with a prison number tattooed on his left arm since 1972, be happy that his daughter - destined to hang around between pots and pans, husband and kids - was joining the police force? How could my mother, who still dreams of settling me down in accordance with tradition, who continues to nag me to find a man with lots of money ("love is for the naive" is her constant refrain), be happy that I'm flying on my own wings instead of submitting to a husband and tradition?

As for Malik...

For the last meal before my departure, he offers me a festival. After singing the traditional anti-cop refrains, he chuckles as my mother serves us chicken.

- At least it's thematic!" he hisses.

He grabs a thigh and disappears into his -our- room like a wolf going to devour its prey away from the pack. My mother tries to talk some sense into him. Barricaded behind the door, he shouts:

- I don't want to eat with that traitor. She's going to work with people who don't like us. She'll learn how to smash her own people without leaving a trace. Doesn't that upset you? Nora, seriously, you have no dignity. Beat it, *mayehbounech*!

As in the ring, when I've taken a good blow, I try not to let anything show. This time, however, I don't have the chance to try a counter-attack. What can I say? My own brother is judging me. And I thought he would at least support me! We've both known for a long time that we had to extricate ourselves from our condition as children of poor immigrants. Barring a catastrophe, I've just found a job for life. In a year's time, I'll have a job. I'll be useful. Not bad, eh?

In any case, nothing to move Malik. I don't know what exactly he's blaming me for. Maybe he doesn't know either. Is it because I'm going to do a job that his friends hate? Is it because, by leaving home for good, I'm signing up for a new rebellion? Is it because being a cop is no job for a woman? Is it because he's jealous of me taking off on new adventures, while he's stuck with a mother who suffocates him? Is it a mixture of these hypotheses? The only truth: I'm sick and sad.

The next day, at 3:30 p.m., I leave to catch my train at Gare de l'Est. My mother insists on accompanying me. As for my father, he doesn't move. Leaning back on the sofa, he barely lets out an almost inaudible *beslema.*

Not a glance.

Don't move.

I don't exist.

To hold this new shock, I try to think of Immanuel Kant, who, in his "Answer to the Question: What is Reason?", sings of "the moment when man emerges from the minority for which he himself is responsible. Minority is the inability to use one's understanding without the help of someone else". When I went to the police academy, much to the chagrin of the usual clichés,

The Philosopher of Barbès

I came out of my intellectual minority. I'm empowering myself. I free myself - in theory at least - from my parents' pre-eminence. I cut the cord.

Beautiful, isn't it? Alas, the Barbès philosopher that I claim to be must admit that, in the face of the terrible grief that overwhelms me, at a time when I should be jubilant at being on my way to my professional destiny, my favorite philosopher is an ineffective antidepressant.

SECOND PART

ROBOCOP

9.

The police academy is an old building that stands on the edge of a forest. This is where I come to face my fears, my hopes and my destiny.

Well-maintained, the building houses two classes of police officers a year, totalling between one hundred and sixty and two hundred trainees. When I arrive, I'm overcome by melancholy, in the sense that Søren Kierkegaard, in *Point de vue sur mon activité d'écrivain,* describes the "inner tonality of the soul" that both elevates us towards God when we feel rejected by men, and separates us from men because it elevates us towards God. My father's indifference - even if it was an extreme expression of the modesty that prevents him from expressing his feelings - shocked me and created in me a lack that is impossible to fill, even today. This is in addition to the feeling of having been abandoned by my parents when my brother was born. In 2020, even though I'm a woman surrounded by many people, often cherished and blessed by her family and children, I can still hear the melody of solitude singing within me, sometimes discreetly, sometimes deafeningly.

In any case, like - or even better than - Kierkegaard (no less!), I know how to put on a good show; and I have to, because there's no room here for mysticism or introspection. On the morning of the first call-up, we all gather in our blue trainee uniforms. The uniform doesn't erase the reality of... uniform recruitment: out of eighty students, there are four of us from the Maghreb, including two girls, and one black. We discover that most of our training will consist of memorizing "memo cards" entitled: "The peacekeeper shall". For example, we're expected to be loyal, impartial and exemplary.

A fine project, on paper! From a deontological point of view, it's beyond reproach. From a pedagogical point of view, it's a little more questionable.

No debates on the program. Few practical cases analyzed afterwards. Very few case studies. No pragmatic reflection on major principles. Lack of time? Deliberate choice? As if intellect were distinct from action. As if, in the police profession, everything didn't come together. As if each element of our training were independent. As if the "sport" module, the "police intervention techniques" (GTIP) module, the "shooting" module, first aid and professional ethics were all separate. As if, more generally, what we are taught could be dissociated from what we experience in the field.

The advantage is that everything is neat and tidy. Nothing sticks out. Honorable ideas mask the bitter complexity that a peace officer faces on a daily basis. This system deprives trainees who are a little out of touch with reality of truly effective preparation; and the institution deprives itself of valuable safeguards.

For example, discussions on social issues such as police violence or illegal immigration could help identify the black sheep that are disfiguring our institution. Titillated by a discourse of concord, haters in general and racists in particular find it hard to restrain themselves. An open conversation would help to detect *wannabe* civil servants whose ideology is likely to harm the police force. Not just to the image of the police: also to their actions, since racist gestures legitimately arouse anger and mistrust among populations who feel oppressed.

Since my training, the greater presence of trainees from recent immigrant backgrounds may have reduced the number of overtly racist remarks. However, it's not certain that microaggressions have diminished in the sense that Sciences Po professor Pap Ndiaye, drawing inspiration from American sociologists, describes them as "little hurtful expressions formulated without necessarily meaning any harm, but stemming from a white ethnocentrism carrying a standardized ideology that can be assimilated to racism" - like when someone says to a black person: "It's hot, you must be happy!", or when someone says to an Arab woman: "You speak French really well!". Even when considered as benevolent clumsiness, these remarks, when repeated, tend to reduce individuals to a particular skin color or religion, which is not acceptable.

Let's be honest: at the beginning of 1998, when I started my training, I wasn't the least bit fascinated by the question. I had a much more essential preoccupation. I'd just met the eye of a 3TBG, a very, very, very handsome boy. As, yippee, he's in my section, I quickly learn that his name is Alex Benmekki. The son of a doctor and a stylist, he has two passions in life: automatic weapons and James Bond. What's more, he has good taste. For example, he's one of the few in our cohort to know that Daft Punk isn't the name of a town in Sweden. And on top of that, he's the only boy I've ever met who naturally talks about cinema, Algerian poetry and politics. And above all, I don't know if I've said it before, he's very, very, very handsome.

Really, really, really beautiful.

More generally speaking, I feel closer to boys than girls. As someone who speaks out against stereotypes, I have to admit that some of them do hold true. For example, when my female counterparts have a day off, they go on a *shopping* spree, avidly seeking out the best manicure to get the "crème de la crème". I, on the other hand, go straight to the boys to work out, box or go drinking beers in the Rue de la Soif, where the bars are concentrated. In the evening, it's the same project: my colleagues compete in sexy nighties, while I'm stuck in soft, ugly striped pyjamas, the ultimate love-killer.

There's no criticism here, just a different choice: despite the "teenage camp" atmosphere typical of any boarding school for young people (but not just young people, I think...), despite the tendency or even the temptation to give in to the facilities of, let's say, temporary endogamy, I'm not at the police academy to show off. If a certain boy turns me on, there's no question of playing the midget. I'm here to learn a trade and build myself up. In concrete terms, what matters to me is to feel good about myself and, by the way, to reveal to the macho guys in the gang the hidden value of hanging out with a chick. Indeed, as a girl, I'm unsuspecting when it comes to defying the school's beer ban. Well, as long as the bottles don't glug too much in my bag...

Apart from that, my real task here is to learn. So, for theory, I swallow the "memo cards". In practice, I repeat the "police intervention techniques", such as arm-locks and handcuffing, which enable us to apprehend offenders as safely as possible, for them as well as for us. And I'm learning my bête noire: shooting.

I remember my first session. We take a bus to the stand. Enthusiastic, some of my companions sang the most beautiful jewels of the occasional repertoire. The horrible "Chauffeur, si t'es champion" and "Jolies colonies de vacances" ring out as I shrivel in on myself... and not even because of the appalling saws bellowed by my peers. What terrifies me is touching a gun. Imagining that, in a split second, I can take away the world's most precious commodity - life - by simply pulling a trigger, bothers me, anguishes me and oppresses me.

It doesn't get any better when, *in situ,* the trainer hands me my gun, a Manhurin F1 (the boys have a heavier weapon). It's classy: silver with a black stock. But it doesn't make me any less uncomfortable. I search in vain for a mirror to take a look. *In retrospect,* I realize how bizarre my reflex was. Nevertheless, at the time, I want to check whether my gun and I are compatible. We've been told so many times that, even if we rarely use it, our gun is our best colleague! In the last resort, it can save our lives. It's our shadow. We must always have it with us. So, I'd like to judge

- if she and I are a match;

- if, thanks to it, I have a chance of inspiring a little more respect in the thugs; or

- if, on the contrary, it makes me look foolish.

An approving look and pout from Alex reassures me. While some of my colleagues are struggling to position their weapons in the *right way* (some of them look like frumpy *cowboys* backstage at the Pinder circus...), I've got the trick down pat. Little did I know that, simultaneously, I had just earned my first police nickname: Nora Croft!

The handsome guy comes over to me. Relaxed as if he was about to sip a coquetèle by the pool of a grand hotel, he sensed that I wasn't 100% in the same *mood.*

- Stressed? he guesses.

- A little.

- Don't worry, you'll see, it'll work. If you want, I'll stand in the next corridor while you shoot.

- Ah, great, thanks...

I bite my lip. How can I, the strong-headed, rebellious, fire-breathing feminist, be such a ninny? Well, there's no mystery: Alex is beautiful *and* kind. Under these conditions, I defy anyone not to melt like snow in the sun when he has the generosity to speak to you.

While basic advice is still echoing ("never point a gun, even an empty one, at someone", "always keep your index finger along the trigger guard"...), we finish fitting out with helmets and goggles. For half an hour, we rehearse the gestures to be performed, and then the instructions click into place:

- Put your weapon into service! Stand up straight! Positions! Nora, your left arm straight, please! Two rounds, shooter! For a shot at five meters, ready?

We can confirm this.

We shoot.

For reasons one can only guess at, I prefer not to specify the result. Nora Croft has her dignity. The brigadier who supervises us doesn't hold it against me for not having put one in the target (well, I specified the result, too bad) because, apart from Alex, we're all at about the same level. As a result, our trainer encourages us and promises rapid progress to those she calls her "children". This woman is one of those trainers who is so caring that you sometimes get the impression she's looking after a nursery. Not the most unpleasant category of instructor, but surprising!

Despite our instructor's reassurance on the way home, I'm not bursting with pride. Luckily, every cloud has a silver lining, and thanks to my failure, Alex comes back to me as we're heading back to school. He tells me that he's a regular at the police shooting range at Porte de la Chapelle. He invites me to join him for a *weekend*. Not at ease with a gun, as you can imagine, I don't feel like prolonging the pleasure when it's slack time! So I politely decline, without ruling out, in my heart of hearts, the possibility of other, slightly more *cosy* rendezvous; and I add:

- In any case, thank you. It's reassuring to be supported.

- It's normal," says Alex with a smile. We have to stick together. It's not going to be an easy year...

- What's your goal after this?

- Eventually, I'd like to join the Renseignements Généraux, but it's hot. They're ultra-selective, and often take on experienced civil servants. But what about you?

- Uh... I'd like to join an anti-crime squad.

- That's it! Dress or civilian?

- Are you kidding? BAC tenue, of course!

Alex bursts out laughing:

- It's only warriors who get a kick out of it...

- That's what I call it. I like action, and I'd like no two days to be the same.

- So the BAC outfit is clearly for you... Are you from Paris too?

- Grave, I lived at the Gare du Nord.

- It's funny, I'm from the seventeenth arrondissement but I went to lycée Jacques-Decourt, just around the corner. Can you see where it is?

- Quite frankly: Antwerp metro, right?

- Exa-act!

- I was three or four stations down, at Colbert, métro Stalingard.

- Crazy!" exclaims Alex. Where, just across the street, was Ticaret, the first *hip-hop* store to open in Europe?

- *Wow*! Ever heard of it?

- We have tons in common, in fact...

He puts his hand on my shoulder, squeezes for too short a time and scurries off to the back of the bus to join his mates. I feel invigorated. Light-headed. In my head, Benjamin Diamond's voice sings the hit of the moment:

I feel right. The music sounds better with you.Love might bring us back together.I feel so good![3]

There's just one downside to the ode to joy that I'm so excited about: a hyperbeautiful kid with whom I share so much can't be single... can he?

---

3. "I feel good. Music sounds better with you / Love will surely bring us together / I feel so good" (Stardust, "Music sounds better with you").

What remains of my first six months as a trainee policewoman are a few scattered memories and two specific scenes.

The first skit takes place in the GTPI class. On this day, we are treated to a role-play situation. A patrol must apprehend the perpetrator of an offence knowingly committed by a trainee. Sub-brigadier Gérald supervises the mock intervention. He sets up the actors, then exclaims with *ad hoc* seriousness:

- Concentrate... Top action!

The police vehicle enters the yard at reduced speed. The plastron colleague throws a garbage can on the road and drives off. The patrol stops him and the first responder, in the style of Marcel Patulaci *aka* Didier Bourdon, calls him out:

- Good morning, sir! Police nationale.

- Hey, man.

- We're going to carry out an identity check.

- From whom?

- From you. Please present us with a...

- Hey, why are you bothering me? I'm working! I don't have time to waste. We don't pay you to bother decent people, do we? Shit, I pay my taxes for you, I never killed anybody, I never ran a red light in my life, and...

- You've just thrown a garbage can onto the public highway," interrupts the driver, who has also got out of the vehicle.

The trainee bursts out laughing:

- Oh, maou! Don't tell me that's what it's for! A garbage can! The National Police for a trash can. Is it me or are you guys just kidding?

- No, we're not messing around, sir. What you've just done is illegal and harmful to the environment.

- Crap! I didn't know the environment commanded the police these days. If I was a minister, would you come and bust my balls over this peccadillo? Are you serious?

- Okay, that's it, you're pissing me off! Come on, show us some ID or we'll take you in.

- Hey! You're going to start talking to me properly, understand?

- Sir," continues the driver, "we've been talking to you properly for some time now, but we're not going to repeat our commands ten times. So, for the third and last time, please show us some form of identification; otherwise, we'll be forced to...

- You've got to be kidding me!" spits the false offender, approaching his colleagues menacingly. That's what everyone does around here when they've missed the garbage round. You must be newbies, but let me tell you something, my little buddies: the Earth doesn't stop turning for all that.

He turns his back on the two officials and says:

- *Ciao* compa...

... when, suddenly, the third colleague leaps out of the car and draws his dummy gun, shouting:

- Don't move, asshole! On the ground, on the ground! Get down! Keep your hands where I can see them! One weird move and I'll shoot, got it?

Flabbergasted, Gérald bursts in and interrupts the exercise by positioning himself right in front of the falsely armed colleague.

- What are you doing?

- Well, I'm calling.

- You're pulling over a gun. For what offence, remind me?

- Throwing rubbish on the public highway, resisting arrest and contempt, tries to support the driver.

A furious look from the trainer nails the two buddies in place. The hysterical trainee holstered his weapon. Stunned, I can only think of one explanation: he had programmed himself for an extreme situation requiring him to draw his weapon. Unable to readjust to the problem, he continued his planning and stuck to what he'd envisaged. So he drew his weapon, knowing no other alternative between a verbal warning and drawing his weapon. In his turn, this slightly dim-witted but no less dangerous coward has earned himself a nickname: Pinot, simple cop. The anti-Aymeric!

The administration, from which we often hear a great deal, doesn't seem to have forgotten the incident. Twenty years later, I ran into this fellow student again. He was behind a desk and had apparently never worked on the public highway. Where he is now, if pushed to the limit of his annoyance, he can throw a Bic or a stapler at an intruder, it's less risky. It's worth pointing out that, from his position, he didn't seem particularly upset.

The second story I'd like to report is worse, although it was supposed to be sweeter! It takes place on a Friday. Friday is the best day of the week, because at 4 p.m. classes end. For most of us, this li-be-ra-ti-on means we're going home.

It's a tradition to get together for a beer in the foyer-bar. Even if I prefer to be out sipping hop juice or more disturbing venoms, I appreciate the opportunity to catch up with friends and colleagues we don't meet for the rest of the week. But this Friday, a surprise awaits me. Brigadier Francis, one of the chief trainers, is sipping his Perrier -which suggests that cops don't have to be alcoholics - and says to me:

- So, Nora, happy to be back with your *smalas* this *weekend*?

Stunned by the term, I frown. My mother, my father, my brother, is that what he calls "my smala"? He continues:

- It's going to be couscous and youyou until Sunday, I imagine! Oh, don't grimace... Deep down, I like you, you know. You were right to join the police. It's better than stealing scooters like the rest of you!

Fear of disciplinary action can't stop me from answering:

- Who, you people?

- Well, people like you...

- Brigadier, I don't know you. I know I haven't got tenure and you're thinking: "I can humiliate her in front of the class, she won't squawk." Bad luck, she'*ll* squawk. You're not my trainer, and even if you were, I wouldn't allow you to talk to me like that.

My cheeks are flushed, but I know the power of these bastards. I don't want to be drawn into a place where there's no turning back - not for him, and certainly not for me. So I pretend to be resuming the conversation with my friends when I hear the last sentence of all:

- Ha, those Arabs... They're all the same! You go off on a rampage for nothing and then complain that we've done you wrong... It's humor, sweetheart. You know what humor is? In France, we're allowed to laugh, I can't help it. So, I'm going to do you a great favor, Nora. I'm going to teach you the most important truth of your school year. If you're Arab and you've got no sense of humor, you can't be a cop. I'm telling you, change your ways!

- I didn't apply for circus school," I reply. *You* know what, Sergeant Francis? Maybe *you're the* one who should change career paths.

- Listen to me, miss....

He frowns and reads my name on the jacket.

- ... mademoiselle Lakheal. I may not be your trainer, but trainers of brainless little girls like you are one big family. Keep provoking your superiors, and I promise you won't finish your probationary year. Do you understand me?

I guess the next few sentences, but Alex drags me out before he's finished. He pulls me against him as I cry with rage at not being allowed to smash that fat bastard's face in.

- Stop it, Nora, he's not worth it. He's a little fascist, a loser. He's taking it out on you because he knows you can't do anything. Calm down! It's not worth getting your spleen in a knot over this idiot. He's impotent, he's a coward... Your life as a cop will prove to him what a piece of shit he is, I guarantee it! And... if you want, Saturday, I'm in Paris. How about a movie?

I nod vigorously, sobbing a little less.

- I'll call you, Nora, I promise. Now, calm down.

A powerful hand rests on my right shoulder. I turn my head. It's Rachida, the daughter of Algerians who grew up in Seine-Saint-Denis. Rachida is not the poet type. The look in her eyes, the way she looks, you can tell that at the slightest provocation, she can go into a tailspin. Especially against the France of yesteryear as she imagines it, *id* like a colonial power, predatory, debasing her homeland. Her resentment is immense. It boils all the time.

Luckily, her intelligence allows her to choose the situations in which she can let her inner rage explode. By becoming a policewoman, she wants to work for a new France. Mixed. Open. The kind that takes shape the moment we meet.

- Don't worry, Nora," she fumes. That son of a bitch, we make him shut up as soon as he comes after us, but he knows we owe him some so-called respect. So, with those who aren't his pupils, he always tries to take advantage of them, the bastard...

- We don't give a damn about him," says the warm voice of Slimane, a Kabyle martial arts champion who's become the darling of our class because he's so serene, *cool* and charismatic. He's a jerk who acts like a kéke in front of students, but he has no experience, nothing. If he were practicing in Stains or La Courneuve, he wouldn't brag so much. Don't worry, you, me, Alex, Rachida and all the others, we're stronger than his *loser* bullshit. Together, we're the future of the police. He's the worst of the past. Nora, we're with you. And it's a good thing you didn't kick the shit out of him. Believe me, he doesn't deserve it.

As I recount these facts, as objectively as I can, an observation strikes me, without arousing any acrimony: I'm surrounded by nothing but Arabs. I don't realize it at the time. I prefer to concentrate on the positive vibes. All the more so as, before Francis came out, no Arab was interested in another Arab because he was an Arab. At no time had this community of origin (which is very flexible, since only a Francis could imagine that an Algerian is *like* a Tunisian) federated. It's rare for "communitarianism" to arise spontaneously. People come together out of affinity, but sometimes a makeshift solidarity is cemented against the hostility of an unjust dominant.

From this misadventure remains a conviction: haters don't deserve our hatred. It's an observation that's stayed with me for the rest of my career. Even though I can still hear those racists screaming in my ears, with their inevitable couplets:

- the worst attacks are carried out by Muslims, look at the Twin Towers;

- among 23 Muslim countries, there is not one democracy, you are savages;

- it's when there are a lot of them that, etc., etc., etc.

In short, for the support, for the lucidity, for the friendship, Alex, Rachida, Slimane, may this book also be the sign of a permanent thank-you to you!

11.

Six months after I started at the police academy, I passed with flying colors. I scored well in all subjects, including legal questions, situational exercises (such as: "As part of a Police secours crew, you're on patrol on the outskirts of a housing estate when you spot a group of young people gathered at the bottom of a tower block likely to be a drug trafficking site. How do you react?") and, above all, sport. Very well trained, I excel in French boxing, where our instructor systematically calls on me to show the group how to perform a particular sequence, move or parry. I'm glad of this, because sports teachers at school are always the friendliest: caring, whatever the student's level... and always ready for a beer after class, which is *the* infallible symptom par excellence!

From now on, I'm supposed to be ready to leave for an internship in the police station of a large eastern city. I'm assigned there with Alex and Recep, a student in the other section of my class. Internships are also an opportunity to meet new colleagues, to broaden our relational network and discover other peers. Recep is a serious and organized boy. In his head, his future is all mapped out. In six months' time, when he finishes school, he'll head off to Turkey to marry his cousin, and then bring his wife to France to start a family. I'm a little distanced by these endogamous traditions, admiring my classmates who already have their life plan in mind... and not unhappy to be, for my part, at the crossroads, with no other plan than to finish the year as well as possible and, afterwards, to envisage a career in the police force in line with my hopes. Committed *and* free, that's all.

One evening, during the course, we reinforce a BAC night team. It's *the* moment I've been waiting for since I decided to wear the uniform. To be out in the field, rubbing shoulders with veterans who are both hotheaded and rigorous - what an honor! But there's a catch: I'm afraid to go out in public with my weapon. "Fear" is not the right word, by the way. I have panic attacks. Going out with a defensive baton and handcuffs is not the same thing as going out with a Manhurin. In the first case, *a priori,* you can't do anything serious. On the other hand, with a weapon, anything is possible. What if I'm forced to draw my weapon? What if I can't get it out when I need to? What if, on the contrary, I'm clumsy and drop it? What if a shot goes off and I hurt someone - I can't imagine anything worse, though I think about it?

There's no way I'm going to get there under such stress. That's why I'm dipping into my Personal Reserve. I've got a pack of Xanax that I stole from my mother one weekend, because I'm so depressed and bored at school. Because, yes, I'm bored here. Sports are fine for five minutes. Beer trips are getting a bit boring. Too often, I meet up with the same people with whom we don't have much to talk about. We make the same jokes over and over again. It's no longer comedy repetition, it's barely repetition at all. What we have in common doesn't go beyond school, our peers and the police, to which we add *soccer,* which I don't give a damn about. Not much to fill the long evenings of "festivity".

In short, yes, I need chemical help. On bad nights, I think I'm going to be stuck here for a year, in this small, limited and limiting universe, and I suffocate. The warrior-ninja-indestructible-fighter shell I've built for myself gets zapped. So, when I'm blue in the face and the combo of sadness + *taedium vitae* + solitude is undermining me, I pull out my secret weapon. A Xanax in the evening, before going to bed and, a good night's sleep later, it's off again!

That evening, everything came together:

- my gun phobia,

- my distress at being confined to a gloomy military base for the internship, and

- the impossibility of talking to anyone about my unhappiness (how can I claim to be a peace officer if I falter on my first serious outing?).

I feel I'm taking a *step forward* in my confusion. So I decide to use my miracle solution. I swallow two tablets in one go on an empty stomach - I haven't been able to swallow anything all day. I'm aware that this isn't necessarily an excellent configuration, but I have no choice.

Finally ready for the BAC outing, I join my colleagues. The brigade leader assembles his teams for roll call. He introduces the trainees to the regulars. We are applauded, then two colleagues guide us to our vehicle... and I feel sick. I feel hot. My cheeks are on fire. I feel nauseous. My head is spinning. My legs give way. I collapse in the police parking lot. Alex catches me mid-fall. In the fog of my mind, I hear him ask Recep to fetch me a glass of water and some sugar.

- A la discrète, hein!" he adds. Hey, Nora, are you okay?

I opine. I'm not talking about the Xanax. I'm just saying I haven't eaten. The colleagues help me to the car and promise we'll buy something on the way. Recep returns. I swallow what he hands me, wedge myself into the back seat and try to hide my discomfort, hoping to recover as soon as possible. If only a major intervention would allow me to show what I'm worth and give a better impression! Unfortunately, luck isn't on my side and nothing happens. The jaded skipper comments to us:

- Well, it's not Paris every day...

We watch the buildings go by, at first on the lookout (ha! jumping up and down on my first outing, that would be great!), then engulfed in a mixture of boredom and disappointment. Suddenly, the radio wakes up: we're needed for a family dispute.

- You see, youth is a sign," says the boss. When you send the BAC to a family dispute, it's because you haven't found much to keep you busy!

For want of anything worse, we arrive at the applicant's home. The house is chic, the neighborhood opulent. Patricia, the woman who requested our assistance, is waiting for us behind the gate of her villa. She's not yet forty. Elegant, she comes from a very well-to-do background. In this painting, one detail stands out: her face. Her eyes are red and still swollen with tears, and a haematoma on her lip is still swelling.

Right away, Patricia wrings her hands and apologizes profusely. She was stupid, she was wrong to call us, she's sorry for... Our boss interrupts the litany to ask, softly and firmly:

- What happened tonight?

- I shouldn't have, uh... So he got a little, shall we say, upset...

- It's not the first time?

- No, but...

- Does this happen often?

The woman grimaces. The dam breaks. Again, tears stream down her cheeks.

- I don't want... anything to happen to her.

Little by little, we get confirmation that Patricia is regularly beaten by her husband. Tonight is just another episode. A habit. So she regrets calling us. The last thing she wants is to upset her husband. He's usually so kind and generous.

- Unfortunately," she adds, "sometimes I'm clumsy. It makes him impulsive, but that's my fault... I'm sorry for the inconvenience.

- Don't you want to tell him to get out and have a little chat?

Patricia paled in panic.

- Oh, no, please, don't!" she whispers at once.

I have the impression that she's on the verge of confiding more. She won't. We won't know if she's afraid for her husband's sake, if she's afraid he'll hit her more in case we switch with him... or if she's even more ashamed, thinking that the neighborhood might be aware that something's wrong with their seemingly perfect neighbors. Our boss takes it in his stride:

- Well, we'll at least take your identity and write a statement. Unless you'd like to file a complaint?

- No, no, no. Really, I'm ashamed to have called you for such a trifle...

- Don't apologize, it's not a trifle," says our boss. That's what we're here for. You were right to call 17. Don't hesitate to do the same if the situation arises again.

A minute later, we're off again, informing dispatch that there will be no further action.

Even though I try not to let it show, I'm overwhelmed with emotion. I'm moved to see a battered woman. Moved by the fact that violence affects all social classes. Moved by the fact that one of my fellow human beings has given up the fight, relying on the law and its representatives. This emotion is my first lesson as a policewoman. We assert that we are not here to judge people; and we assert that we must respect everyone's choices. It's true and terribly difficult.

The realization of our powerlessness and the ensuing frustration have stunned us, and not just the trainees. In the cockpit, no one says a word. We brood over our uselessness and think, in spite of ourselves, of Patricia's worrying future.

A second call dispels our torpor. The radio informs us that a young North African man is lying on the ground with gunshot wounds. He had been spotted in a suburban housing estate. Although the area is not reputed to be dangerous, we call for reinforcements and head for the spot. This time, I'm in the *game*. I'd almost forgotten I was carrying a gun. My unease and discomfort have evaporated. This is what I joined the police force for: to drive at high speed, surrounded by colleagues on the beat, the blue turning on the roof and the two-tone screaming. I shudder. Starsky and Hutch better watch out, Nora and her gang are in the house!

On the spot, we understand that reinforcements will be useless. The area is quiet. The victim is a tall teenager who seems to have ended his life by shooting himself in the heart. To carry out his act, he placed himself behind a pavilion, out of sight. The body is still warm. The suicide was recent. The fire department confirms that the boy is indeed dead. I stare at my first corpse. As a civil servant, the only tribute I can pay him is to treat him with respect. Yet I quickly turn away. Seeing him, I think of my brother. This will be the second lesson of this BAC outing: I'll have to learn to project myself less. To treat the applicants as we would like to be treated our nearest and dearest, yes; but to identify them with our intimates, no. I still have to work on this paradox. I still have to work on this paradox.

I'm shaken but not knocked down. I lack experience? What could be more natural? I'm not armored yet? Well, how can I be? I'm a trainee, I need to get to grips with the reality of the job. That's what internships are for - to help us measure the distance between theory and practice. No book or lecture can prepare us for the realities of our work. Only the field can prepare you for the field. So I'm going to have to find my place and, first and foremost, manage my emotions. Not just for myself. For others. My analysis has taught me that those who are suffering need a calming listener. My first trip with BAC wasn't brilliant, but it was extremely instructive. It has shown me some areas for improvement over the next six months... and throughout the career that, God forbid, will follow.

12.

Six months later, the end of school is imminent. I now know that to know is to ignore. There's nothing philosophical here, just the simple experience of a trainee who, each time she's confronted with the field, discovers how far there is from cup to lip, from teaching to practice, from knowledge to mastery. Like artists and athletes, police officers are aware that the *gap* between being ready on paper and performing IRL can be gigantic.

In addition to learning the basics of the peace officer's job, my twelve months at school were full of astonishing human experiences. For example, after discovering that Paris doesn't stop at the borders of my neighborhood, I realized - incredibly - that France doesn't stop at Paris. No choice... In my graduating class, I'm mainly surrounded by people from the provinces. But in 1998, I realized that mentalities, habits and references were very different between the capital and its outskirts. After a period of adjustment, I think it's great. More generally, boarding school is gradually freeing me from the snobbery intrinsic to the inveterate Parisian. As a result, it's helping me to curb my reductive reflex of classifying people according to whether or not they share my interests. It's not a question of denying my cultures, my particularities, my thirst for discovery or my desire to surpass myself;

but it was important for me to shake up my representations and discover other systems of thought.

I like Bernard Lahire's idea that "sociological determinism is not reducible to determinism by social milieu" (in other words, poverty or wealth influences but is not enough to explain the cultural practices of each individual).

> True sociological determinism brings into play the embodied social [how we've been specifically educated, for example, whether we're a boy or a girl, an only child or from a large family, etc.] and the relational, practical and institutional contexts within which the embodied social is led to actualize itself.[4]

In other words, we are not fixed in the behaviours and habits we have learned. We can - and do - always benefit from allowing our own standards and inclinations to rub up against those of others, so as to question them, bend them and enrich them.

Although...

Declarations of intent aside, the truth is that enrichment through socializing doesn't always work.

Far, far away.

Here I must address the black spot of police culture: karaoke night. Admittedly, I spend my life arguing for tolerance; that notwithstanding, karaoke night in general, and with cops in particular, is beyond the clichés the beaufitude of our institution is capable of conveying. How can I describe it? It's a disaster, an

---

4. Bernard Lahire, *La Culture des individus. Dissonances culturelles et distinction de soi*, La Découverte, "Textes à l'appui / Laboratoire des sciences sociales", 2004, p. 731.

ordeal, a mistake that neither nature nor culture should have allowed. Even the braying about Michel Sardou's "Les Lacs du Connemara" is nothing compared to the rewriting of the musical *Notre-Dame de Paris, feat.* the inevitable: "Il est venu le temps des biteuh de chevaaaaleuh...".

So, with a few colleagues, on the occasion of the last evening, we decide it's time to revolt and troll this obligation. We secede and launch a counter-party. Just before the worst happens, we crank up Daft Punk's anthem "Around the World", which we mix with "Alaoui" by the Orchestre National de Barbès. Of course, some fundamentalist karaokists take offence at our disrespect for tradition. What right do we have to stop them bellowing Guy Marchand's "Destinée" for the umpteenth time? Perhaps some of them have mentally prepared themselves for this sublime moment of communion between peers...

And yet, it's hard to resist the lively music we're pumping out, or our enthusiasm, between impromptu choreography and wild youyous. Most of our comrades join us, beaming, as if they'd had a revelation: they'd never imagined it was possible to free themselves from the traditional ordeal! As a result, all that remains of this real party is one solid regret: that Brigadier Francis isn't there to shake shoulders with the whole prom - minus a few inevitable buggers of bad composition - or, *at the very least,* to see us shake to the music of the rastaquouères from my neighborhood (rpz Barbès, si si!)...

All the more so as the end of our year is a happy prelude to our new life. Which, for me, is starting off rather badly.

I found out about my assignment. I'm disappointed. In order to "rebalance the distribution of civil servants and make up for the shortage of personnel responsible for guarding public buildings", I'm going to help secure the Préfecture de Police in Paris, right across from 36, quai des Orfèvres, where the BRI was nestled at the time. Taking in the news (let's not gibber, I'm crushed), I try to make the best of it by inventing reasons not to be too upset.

- I had little chance of directly obtaining the positions I coveted.

- My task must be carried out by someone. And

- It's just the start of my career, I've got my whole life ahead of me to evolve and get closer to my dreams!

Up until then, the important thing was to get through the training course and come out of it in good standing - contract fulfilled. Now I have to wait until I can be the policewoman I dreamed of being.

A few days later, the end-of-year ceremony brings us all together, in full dress and at attention, in the school's main courtyard. No more shimmying to oriental rhythms. The Prefect himself comes to affix our badges to our jackets and solemnly greets us. The idea crosses my mind that, perhaps, for him, this is a *pensum* he could do without. For me, it's a great source of pride. I feel like I'm in an American movie. The sound of the colors and the Marseillaise swell my chest.

Nevertheless, the soufflet fell when I realized that my father hadn't turned up. I feel betrayed. I'm a little kid who's invested himself in a show, even if he's not the lead, and I realize that Dad hasn't turned up. I feel immeasurable sorrow. A violent wrench. A lion's tooth tears at my heart. It's not his fault, mind you:

- Ahmed had a headache," says my mother, who came along.

As I spot him in the crowd, I try to convince myself that I should at least be happy about this. So I try to read the pride in his eyes.

But to no avail. Either my mother isn't proud of her daughter, or she's skilfully concealing her emotion.

And yet, it was in the family apartment that I chose to start my professional life. There are at least three reasons for this.

- No time to look for accommodation.

- Few resources. And

- I have to keep an eye on Malik.

My mother found her a replacement in a big hotel near the Gare du Nord. She worked as a chambermaid from 2pm to 11pm for €1,280 gross per month. Thanks to her, Malik entered the world of work. He serves breakfast, sets up the rooms and makes sure the housekeeping follows. His trial period was conclusive; he signed a permanent contract. I can just see him in his black pants and burgundy jacket emblazoned with the hotel logo. Perhaps he's found his calling. However, knowing him inside out, I prefer to err on the side of caution.

At work, I discover that there are eight of us "school leavers" at the Prefecture, divided into different brigades. My boss is fifty-five. From the outset, he gives off a good-natured impression that's not contradicted by his demeanor, which combines professional rigor with benevolence.

We work one week in the morning, one week in the afternoon. We take it in turns to keep an eye on various points that are presented as crucial. We have to be impeccably dressed and not hesitate to give information to the people who come to us. We work for the Prefect, who is presented to us as a strict and demanding man.

A tall, lanky colleague in his thirties comes up to me at the end of the welcome speech.

- Hi, I'm Mathieu!

- Nora.

- You've come to the right place. The boss is great, and the colleagues are mostly young like us, so it's *cool*. There are just two little black spots to watch out for: an alcoholic who's retiring in six months, and a fascist, the boss's assistant, who's a 100% guaranteed jerk on invoice.

- Oh, no! Not another fascist!

- Take advantage, there's only one in our department...

With Mathieu, I was immediately hooked. I like the way he's direct and out of the box. For example, you can even make out a discreet piercing on his tongue. For a guard with the Paris police force, that's wickedly subversive!

I discover that, beneath his affable exterior, this elegant dandy is a rebel. His family's hopes of him becoming a great lawyer were dashed. He preferred to become a cop "to piss off" his parents. He works seriously, as I'll see, but his real life is elsewhere, in the Marais, where he has an apartment and a community of friends. When the work is done, the fiesta and the fun can begin. I feel invigorated by his quiet hedonism, even if our professional ambitions differ. Being around someone who's happy, carefree and happy to be alive is a welcome change from my eternal tendency to jump from one worry to another...

Buoyed by her enthusiasm, I rush off at the end of the day to share my joy with my parents and tell them all about my day. My father remains unmoved. My mother is happy. I'm a civil servant, I've got a menial, low-risk job; in short, I'm going to be a marriageable maid again. I'm about to be overcome with dismay when, suddenly, Malik enters the apartment, overexcited:

- Hey, you know what, I was sitting in the square of Saint-Vincent-de Paul, with Toufik and Ridha. We were drinking Coke...

I sneer. In and on my brother's tongue, Coke means whisky. The Coke is there to get the taste across.

- Let me go, you, I'm telling you! We're just sitting there when a bearded guy comes up to us. A pure one, with the fez and all. And then he starts doing his sketch, you know: "Come back to the right path, Allah is merciful", nanani, nanana. The guy was really into *it*! After a while, he got on my nerves, so I said: "Go home to your mother and shave, *khouya*! This ain't no carnival!"

- You were right, my son," says my father. These fools think they can call us *koufars* because they're good Muslims because they have beards...

- Wait, don't you know any better? Toufik, he sees the guy a little surprised by my reaction. Result, you know Toufik, he adds a layer. He hands him a glass...

- ... of Coke, I said.

- Yeah, well, a bit of Coke, normally, otherwise Coke's disgusting. And he said, "Come on, have a drink, it'll loosen you up, bro! We died laughing, and the guy took off. Can you believe it?

- Toufik did the right thing too," concluded my father. Now, everyone out of the living room, *The A-Team* begins...

My father is a simple man. He likes TV series and common sense. Today, when you shake a plane tree, ten bearded men fall out. Back then, that was a rarity. Yet, from the outset, my father had the intuition that these *khouanajiya*, far from bringing emancipation and peace of heart in Allah, were malicious. I wish he'd known and rejoiced that his pertinent vision of the "bearded ones" continues to guide my life to this day.

For the moment, I'm far away from stories about bearded men.

In my booth on boulevard du Palais, I wait for a question from a Chinese tourist, then give him the greeting he's so used to at school and play GPS lady. In fact, most of the time, I'm giving information to Chinese tourists looking for the Sainte Chapelle (opposite) or the Notre-Dame (next door). As a good police officer, I try to be polite and pleasant. Especially since, when I'm not acting as a brief tourist guide, I get bored. Soon, I try to fool my sense of uselessness by evading prohibitions - for example, I rebel by bringing in a little radio to help me wait while I listen to low-volume music.

From where I stand, I can see the prostitutes being brought in or summoned by colleagues from the Brigade de Répression du Proxénétisme at 3, rue de Lutèce. I can see their bodies scarred by abuse - from pimps, clients and themselves, "just to keep up". I make good contacts with one of them, Amina. At the time, this Algerian was in her fifties. Having arrived in France in 1961, she worked as a prostitute to survive until the 1980s, when she married a bar owner in Barbès. A messy divorce put her back on the streets. By the time I meet her, she's fighting bravely to earn enough to bring up her two children and pretend, for their sake, that all is well. I remember her sad smile when, before her chaotic life took her elsewhere, she whispered to me:

- Remain a flower, Nora, and, as the poet Roumi said, offer your most beautiful perfume even to the one who crushes you.

The one that crushes me is my uninteresting work. To give it my best perfume, I try to galvanize myself by looking at 36, quai des Orfèvres. The building crystallizes my ambitions. Symbolizes them. Reactivates them when doubt invades. Often, then. I have to hold on as long as necessary. Find all the subterfuges I can while waiting for my destiny, like Prince Charming, to embrace me and wake me up, giving my existence a little more excitement.

Some days, I'm assigned to the first floor of the prefect's apartment. When the doorbell rings, wearing white gloves and a shiny coat of arms, I have to greet the senior civil servant as he comes down the stairs, in a pompous ceremony, and open the door for him. Most of the time, I just hang around, rereading Immanuel Kant's *Critique of Pure Reason.* The dialectic my favorite philosopher constructs between intuition, experience and knowledge stimulates me intellectually and speaks to me beyond the transcendental reasoning that underpins it. Such is the case at the start of the first part, where Kant challenges the reader.

> Outwardly, time cannot be intuited, any more
> than space can be intuited as something within us.
> So what are space and time? Are they real?

I have the impression that this questioning describes my professional situation exactly. I'm geographically close to 36, but symbolically far from it - as if space were a mere illusion. So I cling to my faith in time and hope to get there one day, telling myself that, later on, if I'm wise and find the opportunity to prove myself,

I'll eventually be able to get closer to these great departments. Ridiculous? Far-fetched? Well, you have to do what you have to do... and my thinking is worth other diversions, like this visit from the major's deputy, who one day asks me:

- Hi, Nora, we've never really seen each other, but... Say, it must seem funny to the Prefect when he sees a rustbucket working downstairs from him!

No time to react, the doorbell rings announcing the arrival of the prefect. Surprised to see two civil servants in front of his house, the representative of the State looks at me quizzically. It's the first time he's been aware of my existence, and I'm surprised by his politeness towards me.

- Are you new, Miss?

- In a way, Mr. Préfet.

- So, welcome," he says benevolently, "and good work."

Apparently, the Prefect didn't mind all that much that an Arab woman opened the door for him. My deputy chief thinks about resuming his inspection tour as if nothing had happened. I catch him by the sleeve and stare at him, whistling:

- Wait a minute, butterfly! You've got a nice Tunisian customs mustache, but you're not my brother.

- I beg your pardon?

- Crouille" comes from *khouya,* the brother. The colonists couldn't pronounce the original word, hence the distortion. But I'm not your sister. Don't ever call me crouille again. Ever again. Ever again. Crouille. Is that clear?

The scoundrel wants to get away. I hold him back for a few seconds, then release him. He tries to compose himself. My exit wasn't in his plans. Nor was mine. The fascist Mathieu had warned me about is red-faced and, I want to believe him, a little worried. I imagine he's thinking that the problem with Arabs is that you can't anticipate their behavior. At any given moment, even when they seem "integrated", these Islamists are capable of the worst. You can't help it, it's in their genes...

- Hey-hey," resolves my N+1, "you look like you've been to school, that's great!

- Thank you, brigadier-chef.

- So, you're going to write me a very detailed report to explain why you're insulting your superior by comparing him to a Tunisian customs officer.

- Perfect. I'll take this opportunity to explain how *you* came to call me a "crumb" in all tranquility. Shall we make an appointment to see who gets the blame?

I hold his gaze until he looks down and turns on his heel.

If this kind of sparkle isn't good for my career, so be it. I have no other option. Gone are the days when, as a trainee, I didn't have to respond to Brigadier Francis' provocations. From now on, I'm not going to let anything get past me.

14.

Apart from this incident, which ultimately had no conse-quences other than the disappearance of the racist deputy from my vicinity, I saw nothing to make my work crisp. Reassuring, but not a good sign. Who joins the police force to feel reassured?

The best times are always lunch breaks. Colleagues are great. We cook for each other. Accompanied by the electro sounds of Jeff Mills, Carl Cox or Moby, we talk about politics, the arts and other little subjects that make life bearable. Until the day when a happy coincidence helps me realize that, insidiously, I'm falling asleep in a comfort far removed from my professional projects.

One morning, I'm on guard facing the Seine and I open the big door for a man. Suddenly, I realize I'm not opening it to a man, but to a *God*. Let's calm down and say: to my idol. To Commissaire Broussard himself. I can't help but salute him and say:

- I know this is unseemly, Commissaire, but I must tell you how much I admire you. You're the ultimate role model for the young peacekeeper that I am.

- Thank you very much, mademoiselle. Where are you posted?

I bite my upper lip and admit, not very proud of myself:

- As you can see, I keep the doors.

- So what's with the sad face? That's what being a policeman is all about!

- True, but I joined the police force to track down offenders, chase them down, jump on them and handcuff them. I'm proud to be useful to our institution. However, the fall is hard...

- There's nothing to stop you from evolving, mademoiselle, please! Ask to leave. I'm sure there's someone out there waiting for you. Help them by being foolish enough to believe in yourself.

The iconic superintendent's smile electrifies me long after he's gone. At the next break, I throw myself at Mathieu to tell him my plan: I'm going to ask for a transfer.

- Why aren't you happy with us?" he wonders.

- We talked about it, Math'. The atmosphere is great, but I want action, and right now...

- We're definitely not RAID... How long have you been here, remind me?

- Six months.

- It's hot! In general, you don't get a new assignment until you've spent a year at a post. But are you a union member?

- Yes.

- It's worth a try, then. It remains to be seen whether the boss will let his darling go...

I laugh at the name and decide to give it a try. What have I got to lose?

The major greets my request with his customary bonhomie.

- I don't really want you to leave us, mademoiselle," he admits. But I won't want to in six months' time, and I'm not the kind of person who holds people back against their will. I'll put in a good word for you.

Thank you. Take care of the report. Tell Sébastien, "my" shop steward. Get on with my life. Open doors. Check bags. See

Robocop

plaintiffs, lawyers, prostitutes, detainees, cleaning ladies go by. Smile. Try to stay alert or pretend I am. Continue my rereading of Immanuel Kant. And, sometimes, I feel a pang in my heart, as when I see a silhouette coming out of a corridor, heading for the airlock, that reminds me of something...

Three-quarter leather, *jeans*, loafers, cold stare, protruding biscottos... It's Aymeric! I immediately press the button that opens the door and turn my head away. I don't want to talk to him again as long as I'm just a plant. He'd think I was a failure and confirm that I definitely don't have the eye of the tiger. I'm not going to disappoint him. I want to see him again later. When I've followed in his footsteps. When I can be proud of having followed the path he laid out for me, fortuitously, one evening after a boxing match at Le Jaurès. I'm not there yet, far from it.

In the meantime, so as not to get too depressed, I'm having a party. Specifically dancing. I've always loved dancing. Yes, in the same way that you can be a rusty and a cop, you can be a nerd who can read Kant in French as a foreign language and a young woman who wants to enjoy life to the full whenever the opportunity arises.

I specifically remember the evening Mathieu turned twenty-six. All the young people in the A brigade were meeting at Wait & See. I was the one who suggested this *spot*, a Parisian mecca for *funk* and *soul*, nestled between République and Oberkampf - a sort of French Soul Train. I love this place. I've hung out there more than a few times. You go there to show off your dancing skills. The best dancers get free drinks - even the rides for grown-ups have their Mickey Mouse tails!

That evening, I'm early. I'm hanging around Place de la République, in front of the Indiana Café. A phone call offers me something to do. It's Sébastien. He tells me what I almost didn't dare hope for. I've been transferred to the central police station in the twentieth arrondissement. I'll be working for Police secours. I'm overjoyed. As I write these lines, I am reminded of the feeling that overwhelms me, and which the Supermen Lovers would sum up a few years later in the first *single* from *Between the Ages*: "All right! OK! Oh, yes! All right!" That's right, sometimes, even an ex-philosophy student has to admit, subtly cadenced with a perfect *groove*, the simplest words are the truest.

I'm a bit sad, too. I know I'll be leaving my colleagues. No need to pretend! If we see each other again, it will be less and less often, until the end, perhaps. The unbreakable bond that unites us will eventually unravel, and that saddens me. I must be worried too: when you change departments, despite the hope that swells in your chest, you know what you're losing, not what you're finding. However, deep down I know I was right to ask for a new assignment. Leaving a quiet position where I could have languished for decades was vital. I can't be content with what I have or what I am. I need to move forward, face new challenges, satisfy my taste for *challenges* and risk-taking.

When the gang gathered around Mathieu, I broke the news. A bit of a shock, as we were getting along so well. A few tequilas and some good music later, the joy and pleasure of being together prevail. Tonight, we have two reasons to celebrate - two more than necessary - and we intend to make the most of them. The worries will wait for us for a few hours, won't they?

15.

In February 2000, I arrived on Rue du Japon feeling more than a little stressed. I feel like I'm diving into the deep end of the pool for the first time. I'm going to be able to see if I can swim... and really do what I became a policewoman to do: serve and protect.

Central 20" is a dilapidated little building, just like in the old TV series I used to watch with my father. I've always believed that, for a policeman, proximity and dilapidation are synonymous with soul and history, sharing and solidarity, modesty and the desire to be useful. Of course, it's more pleasant to work in a clean, welcoming environment. Nevertheless, I suspect that behind these peeling, faded paintwork and damaged furniture lie some beautiful or painful experiences, some of whose mysteries I may soon unravel, and to which I, in turn, will add new stigmas.

In the entrance hall, a tall black man greets me with a tired smile.

- Have you been punished?" he asks.

- Why?

- Nobody volunteers to come to the last arrondissement of Paris, *miss*!

- That's fine by me.

- So welcome home, and good luck!

- Are you the new girl?" a senior officer calls out to me from the corridor. I'm the officer in charge of your brigade. Your changing room is at the end of the corridor. Go and change into your uniforms, your Police Rescue crew is waiting for you downstairs. If you have any questions, don't hesitate. Otherwise, off you go to join your colleagues!

I don't need to be told twice, I'm off.

That's it, I'm no longer an orderly, I'm a cop, a real one, in a car, with a team dedicated to restoring peace and safety, if not on the planet, at least in the twentieth arrondissement (I've got to start somewhere). At least, that's how I imagine it when the radio crackles.

- PS 231 from TN 20.

- TN 20, transmit.

At that moment, I think I've never been so ready in my life to save France by going after a hyper-dangerous thug on the run. The voice of the dispatcher dashed my hopes:

- PS 231, you are called to a water leak at 6, rue Sorbier.

Apparently, water is falling at a private home. His upstairs neighbor is away on vacation. We're needed to allow the syndic access to the apartment from which the water is leaking. Once again, my hopes of becoming a Broussard-style superhero were dashed. All the more so as, on the spot, the intervention, as tedious as it is tedious, seems to take me a long time...

Luckily, when we return to the vehicle, we have a new mission: at 19, rue Pelleport, no one is answering our calls.

- Oh, no," sighs a colleague, no more enthusiastic than that. I hope it's fresh!

Our captain tells me:

- When someone doesn't answer the phone, chances are it's someone who's dead. And, sometimes, the person has been dead for several weeks, which isn't a pretty sight... or smell.

Robocop

In fact, it was the smell that drew the neighborhood's attention.

On the spot, my colleagues put some Vicks in their nostrils to cut themselves off from the stench that greets us. A grumpy cop reluctantly hands me his jar, pointing out:

- First and last time. I'm not Mother Teresa, either. Tomorrow you get yours.

The guys seem nice. I can't wait to have a chance to prove myself to them!

We enter the house. At the far end of the apartment, in the half-light, we make out a body lying on the floor. Despite our protection in the nostrils, the infection is unbearable. A colleague opens the curtains. A vision of horror seizes me. The body is still moving. Hundreds of tiny worms squirm inside. I lean against a wall to hold on. "My second death, after the suicide, is horrible. *The* dead *man* reminds me *of* death, that is, of what awaits me sooner or later, once I've breathed my last. It's a far cry from the corpses pampered by the funeral parlour.

Seeing the photos on the bedside table (probably of the dead woman twenty years earlier, surrounded by her loved ones), I am seized with sadness and think of the "solitude of the dying" described by Norbert Elias. He explains that modern societies have been marked by a significant increase in life expectancy. As a result, death, once commonplace and taken care of by religious beliefs, has become as shameful as it is frightening, especially when religious practice is declining. Since this mutation became apparent, we have tended to hide both the reality of aging and the reality of our finitude. As a result, when, like me, you're not prepared for it (how could you be?), contemplating a decomposing body is a spectacle that's even more violent than it is horrifying.

I fight my stupor by trying to concentrate on what this person was, and by telling myself that, in a way, her ordeal is over. She can be buried with dignity. To claim that this positive thought is enough to make me feel better would be an exaggeration...

When the doctor and colleagues arrive, we leave the apartment without asking for a second thought. I realize once again that I'm going to have to armor myself. Vicks helps with the stench of putrefaction, but it doesn't protect the mind from the shocking visions to which a policeman is inevitably exposed. Only experience will help me find the right compromise between distance and compassion, indifference and projection, insensitivity and over-investment.

16.

Intervention after intervention, day after day, I'm trying to find my feet.

First of all, my rhythm: one week in the morning, one week in the afternoon.

Then there's my equipment: in a case, I store

- templates for drawing up diagrams in the event of road accidents,

- a sharp pencil,

- an eraser,

- a rule,

- plastic gloves,

- a green ticket booklet,

- a notepad,

- a pen,

- a bottle of water,

- Vicks to avoid asking Mother Teresa for help, and, given the lack of chemistry I have with my colleagues,

- a little book that's easier to read in snatches than hard philosophy - I opt for *The Little Prince.*

To really find my feet, I'm also looking for my own place to live. I've submitted a request to the Préfecture. Sharing a room with my brother, not being able to invite people over, not being able to drink alcohol, having to be accountable and feeling like a nuisance no matter what I do or don't do, it's not going to last. With my staggered hours, I'm disrupting my parents' sacrosanct habits. Above all, living with Malik is becoming difficult. Because we're grown-ups and living in the same room is a burden for both of us. And because I've made a point of taking Malik, who's still my little brother despite his size, between the eyes, to tell him to "watch out" when he goes out.

- For the record, I patrol the twentieth," I pointed out.

- What's the big deal? Am I supposed to be impressed?

- Avoid going there to do your bullshit.

- I ain't bullshitting! What the hell?

- I'm just saying I wouldn't want to have to control you.

- But I'm *not* doing anything stupid, are you listening to me or what? So, why do you want to control me? Because I look like a redneck, don't I? Since you betrayed me, you've become the queen of spot checks?

- We don't do racial profiling, Malik, stop it!

- Oh yeah? Like you don't always control the same guys?

- Well, when you know people a little, you know that some guys, every other time, have something to reproach themselves for. So, yes, they're checked more often than others, if that's what you mean.

- How can you talk like that? Anyway, it's better if we don't talk together, right? We've got nothing more to say to each other. You make me so ashamed...

- Me? I'm embarrassing you?

- Yeah, you put me to shame. Can you imagine? I have to hide what you're up to from my friends!

- Really? Why do you ask?

- Their sisters are the real deal. They're married, they've got kids, and when they have to work, they work as chicks.

- Go on, how do you define "a chick's job"?

- I don't know! Secretary, saleswoman, cashier... At least not a cop. A cop's not a woman's job, and certainly not an Arab woman's job.

- Nah, actually, you were right, Malik: when you go on that kind of stupid *trip*, we've got nothing to talk about. On the other hand, you can rest assured that if I come across you and your mates smoking in our area, I'll be checking you out straight away. It won't make me happy, but there won't be any siblings, you're warned.

- Unbelievable! Can you hear yourself? They've filled your head! You feel like you know everything when you've seen nothing! You'll see when you get out to the projects, you'll start to understand what's really going on. It'll do you good, I swear.

I shake my head, sigh and turn away. End of discussion. I've said what I had to say, and I'm sure that underneath his bravado and provocative exterior, Malik got my message.

For my part, I received one, in the form of a text message: the housing office of the Préfecture de Police is offering me the chance to visit an apartment on rue de Chartres, in the Goutte-d'Or district of Paris. I'm well aware of the neighborhood's reputation as a cut-throat area, but I'm in a good position to know that this is a ridiculous exaggeration. It's true that drug trafficking thrives there. Certainly, snatch-and-grab thefts occur. Admittedly, the population may not have the same habits as in the capital's middle-class neighborhoods. But I've never felt unsafe there!

The colorful eighteenth is my childhood. It's the cinema sessions at the Louxor with my father, when a ticket cost five francs. It's the mornings on rue des Islettes listening to "Africa K7" cassettes to discover the latest raï releases. It's the Hamdane brothers' butcher shop and the stalls of the Barbès market, where a three-franc kilo of bananas could be reduced to one franc if you won a verbal joust full of uncompromising *punchlines. This is* the atmosphere described by Rachid Taha in "Barbès": a working-class, cosmopolitan district, full of bars populated by astonishing figures, loudmouths, prostitutes, families, dwellers... Okay, contrary to what the singer claims, I'm not sure there are "never any problems"; but I am certain that this district has nothing of the Far West promised and promoted by hatemongers.

I make an appointment with the janitor and head off to see the place. Bright, refurbished and ready to move into, it's the place for me. The janitor is surprised by my enthusiasm. He doesn't know that, by accepting this rental offer, I'm hoping to find a space of my own where I can build a life of my own and live, alongside my life as a policewoman, my life as a woman. At last!

17.

My professional life starts to take off in the afternoons - from 2 to 8 p.m. - which are considered to be the most interesting because they're the most hectic. Colleagues work in clans, and I've realized that I'm not welcome in my new brigade. I couldn't care less. I'm not going to the station to make friends. Just action and a sense of purpose.

For my debut on the afternoon Police secours shift, I remember an alarm at a convenience store on Boulevard Davout. We were called by the owner. His security guard had intercepted an individual convinced of theft. I'm not too keen to intervene. Someone stealing for food is as understandable as it is reprehensible, isn't it? When we arrive on the scene, the customers' gazes are scornful, even hostile. Indifferent to this electric atmosphere, the security guard leads us into a small room where the store manager and the perpetrator of the theft await us.

The accused is a 1.80 m tall punk. He doesn't steal for food, but to whistle free beer. Blue-eyed, with a not-so-clean but sophisticated appearance, he's rather classy like his peers sometimes seen in New Order clips. Years later, as I write these lines, I'm reminded of "Singularity", one of New Order's "punk clips", whose text seems to me to echo this character:

Winter came so soon,And summer never happened.We're players on a stageWith roles already scripted.[5]

Brigadier Simon, our team leader, sighs as he takes in the scene. He addresses the punk, saying:

- So, you stole some beers, did you? Got enough to pay for them so we can move on?

- Are you stupid?" retorts the interpellée. If I had money, do you think I'd steal?

Dry, my colleague turns to the manager.

- Did you pick up the merchandise?

- Yes, but...

- Because, frankly, taking a guy into custody for two beers...

- Look, I don't usually bother you with this kind of stuff. But this one, I can't take it anymore. He's a regular nuisance in my store. If I don't lodge a complaint this time, he'll be back in a hurry, with all his entourage, and that won't do...

- I can see that. Come on, we're not wasting time. Christopher, pinch the gentleman. Nora, you take the news. We'll get the speedboat on board and you'll come and file a complaint as soon as possible, got it?

The boss nods. Under the punk's thunderous insults, we follow orders. As soon as we leave the room to cross the store, the individual starts shouting:

- Help! This is an arbitrary arrest! Please help me! Police violence! Police everywhere, justice nowhere! Denounce what you see!

---

51. "Winter came so suddenly, / and summer never arrived. / We're playing on a stage / where our roles are already set."

Robocop

Impassive and authoritarian, Christopher leads our client into the car. Less used to this than he is, I feel like pressing "Pause" to explain to those watching us, shocked, dismayed, sure to be witnessing yet another illustration of police arbitrariness, that the defendant is a thief and that we're trying to treat him with the respect and rigor that are our duty in all circumstances... even when they don't make things easy for us. Of course, that's out of the question. I keep my head on straight. Yet deep down inside, I feel humiliated.

So, in silence, I brood over my sadness at having been booed, while we've already headed for the police station's Service Accueil Recherche Investigation Judiciaire (SARIJ). On the way, Brigadier Simon, seated to the right of the driver, turns to the punk and stares into his eyes.

- You know what's stopping me, right now, from sticking my head in your face like a gas meter? Shut up, I'm going to enlighten you: nothing. If I want, I'll stop the car, headbutt you and explain that you threatened my teammate and that I had to react in a hurry. I guarantee you, your mother will never recognize you again. I'm not gonna lie to you, I don't want to. Except that, if I stoop to that, you've won. So I won't give you this gift. You'll keep the same stupid face until the end. I won't touch a hair on your head, I swear.

Stunned by this lesson in morality (and police ethics!), the offender remains stunned. From now on, he wears *a* sheepish expression incompatible with his rebellious appearance. And he murmurs:

- I'm sorry, sir. It wasn't you personally. I was upset, and...

With a gesture, the brigadier cuts him off.

- I don't want to argue with you," he thunders. I've only got a few more words to say to you before I leave you in the lurch. You're twenty years old, you little prick, you stink of death so bad it's an atrocity, and you can't afford to buy your beer from tox. So, in your cage, later on, when you're shitting yourself like a dead rat and you're craving it, try to find two or three neurons in your noggin, and think about the "shit cop" you insulted. While you're rotting in your filthy cell, the "shit cop" will have finished his job and will be enjoying life. So, a word of advice: when your colleagues let you go, go back to your cave and stop busting our balls!

The brigadier turns away and, straight as an I, concentrates on the road ahead. Thanks to his two tirades, I have to say: if not my friendship, Simon has earned my esteem.

The punk pivots toward me. If he's counting on my support, he can always run. I'm still brooding over my humiliation. I'm not ready to forgive him for his little skit. For him, it's just routine comedy with no consequences. For us, this behavior damages our image and makes it harder to practice. His antics contribute to the belief that police exactions are the rule and not the exception... even if a minimum of reflection and good faith would allow everyone to realize that the police are not a barbaric and undignified militia.

When we've handed over the little thief to our colleagues, I take advantage of the break to meet some of my fellow islanders: Erwan le Breton, Stéphane le Corse and Édouard le Picard. These three are proud of their origins and their non-parisianity because, according to them, the capital is the worst place on earth. The air is unbreathable; the streets are as dirty as they are noisy; the people are unpleasant and aggressive. These provincials are just waiting for one thing - to get back to their little paradise, or supposed paradise! So the question of my origins comes up.

- I'm from the Paris region," I say to bury the subject.

- Nah, but where are you really from? insists Stéphane.

- Well, I'm from Barbès.

- OK, but more precisely? Tunisia? Algeria? Morocco?

- Just Île-de-France, in France. Would you like to see my identity card?

Édouard bursts out laughing:

- Hey, it's *great to* have a newcomer like you with us. I hope you'll join our group soon! You've got character and a sense of humor, and that's what we're waiting for. And, without bragging, if you want to discover the borough and its inhabitants, we're the specialists, not your little friends of the moment. We're police on a human scale. I'm sure you'd love that.

- We'll see about that later! I've just arrived, and...

- Nora, we're off!" Simon calls out to me from the door of the break room.

Édouard turns to Stéphane and wonders:

- Did you see how scared they were that she'd be blown away? That chick must be something!

The three of them burst out laughing. Maybe, indeed, I'd enjoy working with these guys...

18.

This time, we're on Rue Buzenval. A lady has called 17 because her neighbor, a notorious alcoholic, won't let her fourteen-year-old daughter named Laure in. Apparently, it's not the first time. We'll have to take a look.

At the bottom of the building, a young girl scratches the asphalt with the tips of her sneakers.

- Laure?" calls Simon through the car door.

The teenager looks up. Wearing a large schoolbag, she has long black hair and big green eyes. She's wearing jeans and a little blue down jacket. She may be fourteen, but you can tell she's still a baby. Simon gets out. I follow.

- Hi, Laure," says the chief. I'm Brigadier Simon. This is Nora. We've come to check on you...

- Ha. Well, I don't know. I got home from school, and Mom wouldn't let me in. So I'm going to take a walk and then wait for tonight. It's okay: Mom's usually tired these days. She doesn't really like me staying at home. She says I bother her. I'd better stay outside.

- Um, we'll make sure she's okay. Where do you live?

- Third floor, right. We can take the elevator but, if you wake her up, I warn you, she won't be happy.

Intervening:

- Don't worry, Laure, she won't tell us anything. Will you come with us?

On the third-floor landing, a pestilential stench jumps out at us. Bad news: Laure points to the door where the stench seems to be coming from. Simon makes up his mind and rings the bell. A dog barks frantically.

- Shut the fuck up, you damn mutt!" a pasty voice grumbles.

Simon immediately rang the bell a second time.

- It's all right, fuck it, I'm coming, we're not at the coins," resumes the stranger. What the hell...

The door finally opens. The stench becomes suffocating. A shaggy guy stands behind the door. He's wearing briefs and seems to be under the influence of a very strong alcoholic state. Between two hills of filth, we see the dog playing with a used sanitary towel.

- Police nationale Can we see the lady who lives here?

- Well, no, she's tired, she's asleep.

- It's five o'clock.

- Yeah, well, she sleeps, doesn't she? She works a lot. Come back tomorrow, maybe, if you've got nothing better to do.

The door slams shut. End of interview.

- You, my little buddy, you're wrong to play this game with me," growls the brigadier half-heartedly.

He looks at me and announces:

- I'll call Central and we'll go to the Minors' Brigade. I'm not leaving the kid with those freaks. You take Laure and put her in the car, okay?

I nod and suggest that the teenager follow me. I smile and explain:

- You were right, your mom was asleep. Who was that gentleman?

- Her new boyfriend. I don't like him.

- Really, why?

- He... I can't tell you but he, uh... he's not... not very nice to me...

Tears stream down her cheeks. She can't go on. Silent sobs shake her. I stop. I look at her, my heart in my throat. I hold out my hand. She takes it. Squeezes it. She is silent. I whisper to her:

- Be strong, Laure. You'll be fine. You're smart and pretty as a picture. Now that we're here, nothing can happen to you! You need a hand, and we're going to give it to you.

- What are you going to do?

- Take you to a place where children are taken care of. Your mom is in no condition to take care of you right now.

- And later I can come back when she's awake and strong again?

Disconcerted, I promise yes, specifying: "Not immediately, when the time comes", as I think the story might be a little more complicated than Laure wants to believe.

A few minutes later, we're off to the Central Brigade of the Regional Criminal Investigation Department, home to the Minors' Protection Brigade. While Simon *briefs* our specialist colleagues, I invite Laure to drink a hot chocolate from the machine.

- Can I ask you a question?" she says, sipping her drink. Was your mom nice to you?

Unprepared for such glue, I prefer to lie to help her anticipate the separation from her mother. So I improvise:

- My mother died when I was little, and I never knew my father.

- Well, how did you do it, then?" she wonders.

With a timid index finger, she points to my uniform.

- I met people who helped me grow. Thanks to them, I was able to become the person I am today. It hasn't always been easy, but... In difficult times, I used to say to myself: "OK, I didn't have two parents who love me, like we're supposed to have. Never mind, I'm sure that nothing's a foregone conclusion. I'll get through this, I swear. With books, I'll break through all the walls." Since then, I've always had a book with me!

- Even when you're a policewoman?

- Why should I? You think the police can't read?

- I didn't say that," she protests.

I open my briefcase and hold up *The Little Prince*. I ask him:

- Have you read this one?

- No.

- Do you want it?

- Oh, yeah!

- It's for you. But be careful! I'm not giving it to you. I'm lending it to you. When you've grown up, you'll come and see me, and we'll talk about everything that's happened to you since we met.

- It'll be a long time before I'm an adult... You'll have forgotten me!

I put a finger under his chin to force him to look up.

- Tell me, Laure, are you accusing me of forgetting my promises?

We stare at each other for a moment. The girl considers my question seriously. Finally, she shakes her head.

- So I'm counting on you.

- Laure, do you want to come with me?" asks an OPJ from the Brigade des mineurs.

I see our protégée's eyes filling with tears again. Without thinking, I take her in my arms and hold her tight. Then I let go and watch her walk off down the corridor with my book.

I don't want to look at the head sergeant waiting for me. A working policewoman doesn't cry. The proof, I don't cry.

When I've finished not crying and I'm strong enough to hold Simon's gaze, I read in it: "It's cute, what you've done, but it's useless, you know..." He's right, no doubt, but I don't want to admit it. I'd rather bet on the future. In that, I haven't changed. I hope to be, once and for all, the policewoman who waits for Laure to return her copy of The *Little Prince.*

19.

That day, I have an appointment with a saber on avenue Gambetta.

To be more precise, just after I took up my duties, we were asked to intervene on Avenue Gambetta, as an individual carrying a Japanese sword was threatening passers-by. Indeed, when we arrived on the wide thoroughfare, a tall black man was strolling down the street with his blade. He's a Rasta in his thirties, dressed in fatigues. He's got a fearsome weapon in his fist and doesn't seem to be kidding at all. Without hesitation, as soon as the car has skidded to a halt, Simon pops up, pistol in hand, and shouts:

- Get down! Get down!

We too jump out of the car. Surprised, the rasta lowers his sword for a moment. Immediately, Christopher pounces on him from behind and rushes him to the ground. With a kick, I push the sword aside and handcuff our target. The guy's in the throes of a mystical delirium, which doesn't make him any less dangerous - on the contrary! - the danger he represents. We bring him back as quickly as possible... and are immediately called in for backup.

Could it be the full moon, which is reputed to put a strain on the systems of psychologically fragile people? Another madman has a seizure on rue Soleillet. We arrive at full speed. Colleagues are on site, setting up a security perimeter. It's a sight worth seeing. The "Dies Irae" from Mozart's *Requiem* resounds. On the third floor, on his balcony, a white man is walking up and down. He's in his thirties, dressed only in briefs and sporting a tuft of tousled hair. When he runs out of ammunition, he goes into his apartment and comes out again with his hands full of dishes.

Aiming at a bystander (one of those we call a CQR for "con qui regarde" - "idiot who stares"), he throws a plate in his direction and lets out a "Voilàààà!" on impact. Then he throws a ramming-pot at a car just outside his house. The windshield explodes.

- Bravoooo!" he roared, doing a little dance of joy.

Then a plate aimed specifically at the police force. Then another. Then another.

- But you're not going to make it, my *friend*! exclaims a colleague who is making progress, taking his time.

His Marseille accent matches his looks. Immediately, go figure, he inspires enormous sympathy. Not just because he's wrapped up: he's got a good head, a funny accent, and looks relaxed in a situation that's both funny and tense. When you put it all together, it makes me want to become his girlfriend. Because although the scene is dangerous (getting hit in the face by a plate thrown at full speed is no laughing matter), it's also hilarious that

- see Culbuto's way...

- ... waddling along...

- ... while a crazy guy in his underwear gets rid of his dishes...

- ... rocking Mozart to the max on his stereo.

Nervousness or awareness of the absurdity of the situation? I burst out laughing. The newcomer turns to me:

- Why are you laughing, colleague?

- Because laughter is the polite expression of the tragic," I said without thinking.

- Good Mother, they're recruiting philosophers into the police force! Poor us! What's your name, pisser?

- Nora. How about you?

- Hakim. Come on, come with me.

- Wait, I didn't tell my bosses, and...

- A guy can kill someone with his crazy projectiles. He can commit suicide by throwing himself off the balcony. We'll stop him. We don't care about the rest. How's that for justification?

I confirmed, happy to finally meet an obviously experienced colleague who deigns to both trust me and take me under his wing.

- Everyone, we're heading for the stairs," he announces. I'll take Basilis and... er, Nora with me.

With Basilis and Hakim, we trot up the stairs (already quite a sprint for our intervention leader!). Arriving at the door where Mozart is thundering like he's never had to thunder in this neighborhood, Hakim knocks firmly and shouts:

- Sir, it's the police. Open the door!

In the wait that follows, I gamble. The individual looks a bit odd and hasn't used a firearm so far, but that doesn't mean he doesn't have one. Perhaps he chose to use it only when the police came to arrest him? We're trying to make out the noises that the music is drowning out. I think I can make out voices. Is it the quartet from "Recordare"? The chorus of "Confutatis"? Could there be more than one inside? Caught up in his crisis, has the plate-thrower hurt a housemate? Annoyed, I in turn knock on the door and loudly demand that the door be opened.

Against all odds, we hear a key turn in the lock. The latch lowers and a gap appears. Trap or surrender? Over the airwaves, our colleagues inform us that a fireman and a policeman are at the top of the large ladder, close to the balcony, ready to intervene on our instructions. Gun in hand, I push the door open to carefully enlarge the opening.

Just then, the first soft bars of "Lacrimosa" sound. At first glance, the apartment is deserted. Where is the Mozartophile hiding? Hakim beckons me to enter first. As I watch him walk past, I realize he's wearing his bulletproof vest. I didn't think to take mine from the car. If I take one, I'll (almost) only have myself to blame!

While Basilis covers us, I follow Hakim into the dwelling. Sobbing seems to be coming from a room at the far left. The man in the briefs is in the bathroom, collapsed under the sink like a pile of dirty laundry. In his hand, a knife. Not phenomenal, but a knife nonetheless.

- Kill me!" he begs, sobbing. Kill me or I'll kill myself!

- It's over, drop your blade," orders Hakim in a loud voice.

- Kill me first, please!

We understand that, by now, the individual, at the end of his rope, has become harmless again. While I keep my Manhurin in my hand just in case, Hakim grabs him by the arm and pulls him up. Spontaneously, the guy drops his knife. He's in no condition to put up any resistance.

- End of intervention, announces Hakim. I repeat: end of intervention. Individual safely under control.

A fireman and a colleague enter through the balcony. We turn off the music, let the man put on a bathrobe and handcuff him.

I'm euphoric. Another successful intervention, and with a nice colleague to boot!

I was right to rejoice in the moment, for a cold shower awaited me. Shortly after this exotic arrest, my brigade boss summons me to inform me that I've been transferred to the islets.

- The current policy is to strengthen contact with the population through urban community policing," he pontificates. None of the J11 members want to go. As you're the last to arrive...

He didn't finish his sentence. What's the point? I bow my head and sigh. When, at last, I feel in tune with my work, I'm forced to change.

- Your new colleagues are waiting for you in the break room," concludes my interlocutor. You're dismissed.

20.

Édouard welcomes me.

- It's good to see you happy to be working with us!" he jokes, noticing my defeated expression.

- You know I'm happy to be working with you... but it's not very pleasant to be thrown out like a piece of trash. I appreciated Police secours, and I don't feel that I've underestimated you!

- Don't worry, we're nice here and we do a good job too. Anyway, no one has ever fit in at J11. They always find a way to push newcomers out. They work well, that's not the point; but they work together, they eat together, they go out together, and I'd rather not know the rest of what they do together. So when someone comes to change their routine, they're not welcome... especially if it's a woman, she's pretty and she's Arab. In their defense, I have to say, you're a serial offender!

Although very sensitive on the subject, I understand that, with Édouard, this notion of "offence" is in no way tinged with racism... and that's regenerating!

- Come on, let's get you into the swing of things.

- What is the program?

- We run a school and then take a stroll around Saint-Blaise, between rue d'Avron and rue de Bagnolet.

- A school point? Is this a joke?

- No, we make it safer for children to cross the road and around schools. It's cute, it lets us get to know people, and it's part of our mission to serve the public. Why do we do it?

- Well... I like action and I get the impression that it doesn't like me. Already, for my first police rescue, I had to deal with a water leak, and now...

Édouard bursts out laughing.

- Be nice, don't kill yourself now! he says. And don't worry, we've got lots of different missions at the islets. We're not as telegenic as the RAID, but you'll soon realize that our work is absolutely essential.

At the time, I wasn't convinced. Today, I'm a firm believer. As proof, after the local police were abolished on the pretext that we spent our time playing *soccer* with the *drug dealers'* little brothers, some people dream of reinstating them because, as Édouard insists:

- We are indispensable to society.

- Well, if we're talking about an indispensable guy, we're talking about me, I guess," says the colleague who joins us.

- Luca, meet the indispensable Nora, and vice versa. Oh, but there's one thing you need to know, indispensable Nora: a neighborhood watchman works a lot. So, tomorrow, forget your regulation shoes and come in dark sneakers.

- Are we allowed?

- Seeing as the boss gives it to us, do you think we're going to go without!

So it's off for the school crossing and then for the "Saint-Blaise stroll". The area is a hotbed of drug trafficking. We're not here to dismantle this big *business*. Rather, we're there to get to know the kids who hang out there, make contacts, glean information and, if need be, put an end to any minor offences we come across. Just as my colleagues are filling me in on what's in store for me, Luca exclaims:

- Look, Édouard, isn't that Cherif's *scooter*?

- I guess so...

- Strange, at this hour, the owner must be asleep...

- Cherif is a small-time *drug dealer*," Édouard tells me. Hey, Moussa's driving! Come on, let's check him out.

Luca steps forward. The *scooter* stops.

- Identity check," announces my colleague.

- Sir, we've been meeting every day for ten years. Why are you arresting me? You know the color of all my underpants!

- So I want to see if you've got a new one... and, incidentally, see what you're carrying. Can you show me?

- I'm not "lugging" anything, sir.

- Did Cherif give you his *scooter* for your looks? Or because you had a home delivery on the agenda?

- Nah, I was just out for a walk, chief, I swear. Just to get some fresh air, that's all. Nice weather, isn't it?

- How long are you going to take me for an idiot?

- I wouldn't dare, no shit. I have far, far too much respect for the police, sir! Besides, it's Friday, so you know you won't find anything on me.

- Why?

- Come on, Friday's the *Sabbath*!

- Aren't you *muslim*?

- Well, it's the same! Come on, let me through...

- Open your *top-case*, instead of yapping. By the way, Nora, Mr. Jacasse's name is Moussa.

- The life of my reum, don't tell me it's not true! glapitated the interested party, overplaying his stupor. Do the cops hire little girls?

I raise my hand:

- Don't give me that. I'm not a damsel. I'm a police officer. Understand?

Without stopping to examine the contents of the *top-case* (Coke, leaflet, nothing more), Luca smiles.

- Yes, Moussa, in the heat of the moment, we didn't have time to tell you," he comments. We're nice people, but the new girl's not to be messed with. How's Samba?

- All right, why?

- Because you're the oldest. You have to take care of your brothers a little more than you do. Set them an example.

- We spoke to your mother yesterday," says Edouard. She's working very hard for you, do you realize that?

Moussa chimes in and replies:

- Don't worry, I can handle it.

Luca closes the *top-case* and signals to Édouard that the inspection is over.

- Say hello to Cherif, will you? concludes the Picard in the group.

- All right, then. Au r'voir, madame!

- See you soon, Moussa.

We watch him walk away, then resume our pedestrian round. As if reading my mind, Édouard puts his hand on my arm and says:

- You're right, Nora. We're useless, but we're useful. You'll see, often, that's much more important.

21.

As on the chicest beaches of the Côte-d'Azur, albeit slightly less glitzy, summer has taken up residence in the twentieth arrondissement.

On this particular afternoon, I'm working with my now-faithful sidekicks Luca and Édouard. My colleagues warn me that summer afternoons are sometimes the hottest, and not just in terms of the thermometer: for a variety of reasons, the temperature can go to your head. Since they've told me this about full moons and lunatics, I can safely assume that - out of kindness - they want to prepare me for the worst. In this way, the whole thing will seem tranquil instead of tedious. What's more, thanks to their warning, I won't imagine that, just because the weather's nice and everyone seems to be smiling, our stroll will be peaceful.

And yet, our tour is shaping up perfectly. My acolytes, connoisseurs of the local fauna, lead me straight to Osiris, a shisha bar on avenue Gambetta. The estaminet is run by Ghazi, an Egyptian who knows a thing or two about what's going on in the area.

- *Too* aware," says Luca as we approach the place. 95% of his stories are bunk, but the other 5% are well worth it. You just have to be there and on your toes when, in the middle of his blather, he reveals the 5% we're interested in...

The owner greets us with a radiant smile. He offers us a mint tea. Despite the heat, we accept greedily... when suddenly, in the street, shouts resound. Immediately, abandoning the promised pleasure, we leave the bar. I see a tall teenage girl beating up a fifty-year-old who, overwhelmed, moans:

- Stop, Fanta, stop...

Powerful and alert, Luca and Édouard leap up and seize the girl to put an end to the aggression. I push aside the victim, who is crying and bleeding. The man has bruises and bites on his neck and hand. I ask:

- Who is this girl?

- *My* daughter. She's angry because I don't give her any money. But the truth is, I don't have any money! I barely get an allowance for my disability, so I can't give her... give her... give her any money...

Dignified as he can be, the man is on the verge of tears. Luca approaches us. It's then that the daughter starts spitting on her father, accompanying her glaviots with her most beautiful repertoire:

- Dirty bastard! Son of a bitch! Fuck you, motherfucker! You're a piece of shit! Die, asshole!

- Pinch her, Nora, we're taking her in," concludes Édouard with his customary calm.

That's one quality I like about him: experience hasn't jaded him, it's polished him. He is not indifferent to the situations he deals with. He's content to approach them more humanistically than phlegmatically. I'd like to have that professional distance, never cold, that he knows how to create between the event to be dealt with and himself.

I approach to handcuff the excited girl. With a sudden movement, the strong girl slips into Edouard's hands. Fearing for her father, I lure her away. She tries to free herself and turns menacingly towards me. I resist. She grabs me back. One sweep later, we fall heavily to the pavement. I manage to grab one of her hands and pinch it, but the other escapes me. With a headbutt, my opponent, taller than me, collides with my lips, which explode. Blood spurts out and enters my nostrils, hindering my breathing. Nevertheless, I hang on to the pest. Edouard intervenes and tackles her to the ground. With his help, I finally manage to subdue the recalcitrant woman. The situation is frozen. Apart from me, things are better.

- Are you happy, you bastard?" says the unimpressed Fanta, turning her head towards her father. You bastard!

- Sir, would you like to lodge a complaint?" asks Luca, with few illusions.

- No, no, she's my daughter... And it's my fault... I don't take good care of her...

- That doesn't give him the right to hit you, or the police officers who come to your aid. Nora?

- I'll live.

- TN 20 d'Ilots Bravo. We're at the bottom of avenue Gambetta. Need a vehicle to apprehend and take to SARIJ a virulent person.

While waiting for reinforcements, I grab the handkerchiefs Ghazi has brought me. Even though, huffing and puffing after the effort, I keep my outward composure, I'm angry.

Angry at the girl who hits her father over money: how can a child lose all common sense like that?

Angry with myself, too: even though Fanta is more massive, I should have managed the handcuffing myself. I conclude that

I'm going to have to train more for this kind of intervention, and I promise myself that I won't miss any more training courses that might help me in this respect.

What's more, twenty years later, I'm angry when I think back on that scene, because I can only imagine what would have happened to us if it had been filmed. What would we have seen? A clumsy young policewoman martyring a black teenager with the help of her white colleague. As with the punk stopped at the Leader Price, I realize how misleading the images are. It's not a question of asserting that no police officer has ever committed violence that is as unjustifiable as it is unjustified - that would be absurd. Rather, it's a matter of pointing out the obvious: if you only show part of the reality, even if you are moved in good faith by the violence of what you see, you can mislead viewers.

All the more so as a video filmed today by a cell phone is connoted, in the sense used by Roland Barthes in *La Rhétorique de l'image (The Rhetoric of the Image)*, *i*.e. it has a meaning that, in a way, pre-exists it. Clearly, whatever the reality of the facts, the very principle of *cop watch* means that if you see a cop video taken in the energy of the moment, in this case that of a complicated handcuffing, you immediately assume that the policeman is guilty.

Except that it fails to show that, the moment before, the woman was hitting her father, spitting at him, threatening him and insulting him.

Except that we also forget to show that this person refused to obey simple, justified commands.

Except that we finally forget to show that, as a bonus, she attacked an officer who had no intention of assaulting her, just of taking her to the safety of a Judicial Police Officer so that she could explain the assault she had committed on the public highway.

All in all, this could have resulted in three unfortunate omissions, unless you want to sink into sensationalism that is as conducive to *buzz* as it is unfair and harmful.

The solution - if not ideal, at least optimal - seems obvious to me: every colleague on every patrol should carry an on-board camera, or *at the very least,* every crew should have one. Personally, when I intervene, I have nothing to hide. I'm neither an example nor a model, I'm just an inexperienced policewoman, but when I wear the uniform, I'm carrying out a mission, I'm acting within the strict framework of my duties and prerogatives, and I'm not mistreating anyone. I'm even the one with exploding lips!

I would therefore gladly accept to be permanently "flipped" (ha, ha). In the event of an intervention being contested, the transparent broadcasting of the entire sequence presented as litigious would restore the probity of honest civil servants. Granted, this equipment would represent a financial cost, but what would that be compared with the considerable gain in terms of image and connection with the bona fide population? From what I've seen, I can say it loud and clear: when they're on duty, very few police officers have anything to hide.

Rare, not non-existent. We'll get to that, alas.

Two hours after the altercation, we've taken Fanta into custody; I've lodged a complaint for rebellion against a law enforcement officer; and, although I feel disfigured because of my injured lip, we're back on patrol. Our shift isn't over yet, and as far as I'm concerned, it takes more than that to get me down!

So we resume our tour with the essential: a break. At a local grocery store, we do a little shopping. While I, a wise young civil servant, treat myself to a brave bottle of water, my more experienced colleagues take it upon themselves to sink into vice. Without hiding, they buy their dose of drugs: a bag of Malabar for one, a packet of Carambar for the other. Watching these two sturdy fellows shoot up with cheap dye and sugar warms my soul. I guess we're all peacekeepers, but we're still human, aren't we?

Moments later, in the Ménilmontant sector, a motocross emerges and rears up in front of us. Two other machines follow... and the trio, obviously not wearing helmets, brushes up against us several times. Édouard reports the rodeo to the other patrols and tells me not to intervene. Too dangerous for us and for the young idiots. Even if we were in a motorized vehicle, what could we do? Chasing them means encouraging them to speed up. But what if, in their flight, they hit a passer-by... or a pole? Letting them run is the least worst solution, and hoping that one of them doesn't have an accident - especially when we're nearby, as we could be accused of causing the tragedy.

In short, I'm ranting, raving, powerless... and that's when a silk-screened car flashes its headlights at us. I approach the driver. I can see he's only got a chevron on his shoulders: he's a trainee. However, when he rolls down the window, I see that it's not just any trainee.

It's the opposite of any trainee.

He's the most beautiful trainee in the galaxy.

It's the incredible Alex Benmekki himself.

In a hurry, we exchange three meaningless words and our telephone numbers, which do matter, and go about our business.

I feel light and refreshed, although I regret having seen my partner with my damaged lips. Didn't he think I was ugly?

I can't help smiling for the rest of our vacation. And I'm always smiling when, in the evening, I see Malik arrive in my Goutte-d'Or apartment, which is more than simply furnished. Apart from a mattress, a few dishes and a coffee maker, my *home sweet home* is deserted.

On the pretext of coming for a coffee, my brother tells me that his release-reconversion is imminent. A client has asked him to apply to become a *steward* with Air Tahiti. I'm delighted and not at all surprised. With his build and looks, he'll look good as an air host! Especially as he promises to have slowed down on the cannabis.

Golden colleagues, Malik out of the woods, Alex around... What more could you ask for? Nothing. Absolutely nothing. Prospects are bright.

However, despite this euphoric impulse, I have my doubts. Unable to ever be 100% fulfilled, I'm wary. I know all too well that, in general, bad surprises only wait for the good news to arrive to remind me that life isn't as simple as I'd sometimes like to believe...

22.

The next day, a special mission awaits us. We have to restore order in a housing estate where a colleague was seriously injured the day before during scuffles that got out of hand. Bullet-proof vests and helmets are a must. We don't get the most exciting part, as six of us find ourselves in a "TC", a minibus, while other colleagues patrol on foot. Our presence must reassure the population, mark our commitment in a place where we're not welcome, and dissuade crowds while we're in the area.

Yet regularly, unimpressed youngsters pass by and taunt us through the window. Édouard gnaws at his brakes.

- Have you seen these little idiots? They've got nothing better to do than hang around looking for trouble. That's the kind of punk who cut the eye of our colleague yesterday, and it pisses me off because when we slip up, we talk about "police blunders", whereas when they mutilate us, there's no word for it. As if, when you're a cop, it's normal to come home crippled from a day's work...

In short, some rant to relieve their boredom, others just doze off. At mid-day, we take turns buying food and stretching our legs. A colleague pulls out a small radio. An hour later, "Starlight" by the Supermen Lovers plays for the fourth time, and we find ourselves singing the chorus at the top of our lungs:

Starlight, can you give me the fame? Can you hurl me the game, oh, starlight?[61]

Phew, that's relaxing! Thanks to this tube, the monotony of our static guard is gradually broken by a beautiful atmosphere.

That's when I see Moussa rush past and hide behind a bush, just opposite Belleville Park. What a waste! A vehicle from J11, my old brigade, rolls up and slams on the brakes with a loud screech. Two colleagues jump out and rush towards the fugitive. Cherif and his mates then appear out of nowhere and start hurling projectiles at our vehicle. We immediately get out, helmets on, to disperse the provocateurs.

Meanwhile, a colleague I don't know caught up with Moussa and threw him to the ground. Now he's beating him with a tonfa. Moussa screams.

- You're not so cocky, are you? barks the colleague. And that's just for starters! You're going to eat the floor, you son of a bitch!

The other youngsters change targets and run to the unfortunate man's aid. The confrontation turns into a pitched battle. Not a specialist in maintaining order, I try to put my opponents on the back foot by drawing my gas… but, in the confusion, I use it badly and, to my great shame, I realize that I'm spraying my team as much as the troublemakers.

When, in spite of my clumsiness, we managed to repel our opponents, Edouard lifted Moussa, who was bleeding profusely, and called out to his colleagues:

- What the fuck is this sketch? Are you nuts?

---

61. "Starlight, couldn't you make me famous / and make things go faster for me?"

- He refused an inspection, the bastard. He's been playing us for fools for years. And Melinda lost an eye yesterday, remember?

- But it's not his fault!

- Stop being such a little bitch, damn it! He took for the others. He'll tell them what it's like when someone breaks our balls. Do you bet that from now on, they'll let go of our underpants?

Édouard is flabbergasted. I'm flabbergasted. Stunned. Stunned. The colleagues on the bus with us say nothing. I want to believe they too are shocked.

This gratuitous, stupid, easy and cowardly revenge is an absolute scandal. It's neither a "blunder" nor a "slip-up": it's a deliberate act by a despicable character who has no place in the police force. There's no angelism in what I'm saying, because I know that Moussa is in cahoots with the local petty dealers; I know that he's involved in *drug dealing* and is in a bad way; we're watching him, we're checking him, we're reprimanding him and, if need be, we'll always be ready to take him back to the station if necessary. On the other hand, the presence of black sheep in our ranks is unbearable. These traitors bring our work into disrepute and put us at risk by throwing oil on the fire. They must be disbarred and punished by the law.

I meet Moussa's eyes. I feel ashamed.

As the J11 boards their prey, Luca tries to comfort me. He advises me not to be so sensitive. He assures me that I'll see more. He tells me I've got to brace myself, because we can't help having guys among us who, when they're on edge, get a bit more violent than they should. I don't answer him. Even the "a little more violent" doesn't make me react. Nothing can justify the "slightly violent" scene I witnessed. It's the only evidence there is. There's no arguing with it.

I can't wait for my shift to end.

23.

As soon as I'm through the checkroom door, I text Alex. We meet at the Blanche metro station, near the Folies Pigalle, a former Mecca of the French touch. I take a seat on the terrace of the bar next to the nightclub. Alex doesn't take long. He looks tired. He thinks I look a bit small. I admit that the job wears me out. Physically and morally. He adds:

- I haven't even been in the game a year, and I'm fed up. I'm sick of chasing after guys to take them into custody... only to find them three hours later, taunting me on the street corner. I feel like I'm doing nothing. So much energy spent for nothing! In the long run, I have to admit, it drains me.

- The same goes for me: I've had enough tonight.

- From?

- Too many things. From jerks. My parents. Everything. In short, I see only one solution.

Alex raises her beautiful eyes to me, a questioning gleam in her eye. I hail the waiter and say:

- Waiter? Two tequilas, please.

- I'll bring it to you!

- Wait!" Alex says to me as the waiter disappears. Isn't this when I'm supposed to add: "Two tequilas for me too"?

I smile at him. He smiles at me. Despite my fatigue, I can't have felt this good very often.

Two hours and a few grams of alcohol in our blood later, our weariness hasn't gone away, but it doesn't matter anymore. Alexis offers to walk me home. I'm dying to... and yet I refuse. I don't want him to see my apartment, which is as empty as my life. Some other time, I hope. Not this time. So, as we part, he takes the initiative and, grabbing me by the chin, offers me our first kiss. Afterwards, I tell myself that if I die tomorrow, it won't matter: I won't have lived in vain.

I walk home, my head in the stars whose light I was singing at lunchtime. Even though I'm alone, the world in general and my worries in particular suddenly seem much more bearable. When you think about it, and my experience attests to this, it wouldn't take much for every human being to be happy: tequila, a kiss from the most beautiful boy in the world, and bingo!

Not for long. On my doorstep, there's Malik.

- Where were you?" he asks in a pasty voice. I've been waiting for you.

- Ben, I'm here. Come on in. What's up?

- Nora, I've got big news for you.

- I'm listening.

- You're looking at the all-time world champion of *losing*...

- ... and a guy who's done his whiskey justice, right?

He staggers off, looking amused.

- Oh, sorry, Mrs. Perfect. I forgot that you never drink!

- What's happened to you? Why did you turn your head upside down?

The tone suddenly changes.

- It's Mum," says Malik, his jaws clenching. She doesn't want me to be a *steward*.

- Huh? Why should I?

- She says I'm not allowed to go too far from home and abandon the family.

- But you don't give up on anyone or anything! You build yourself, you live your life, you grow!

- Still, if something happens to the two of them and I'm on the other side of the world, what happens, right? Can you tell me?

- Yes: I'll be there. Just as I've always been there when there's been a problem.

- Nah, you're different.

- In what sense?

- You're too late. You've abandoned us. You left like the selfish bitch you are. So now it's just me. I'm forced to stay with my parents and keep my shitty job. Thanks to who?

He points his index finger at me.

- Thank you, Nora," he captioned. Because, really, it's not Mom's fault. It's yours.

I sigh and dot my I's:

- Malik, it's nobody's fault. No one's forcing you to stick by your parents, just as no one's forcing you to drink and smoke. Stop kidding yourself. Pull yourself together, for God's sake, and stop listening to Mum's whining. You know what she's like! One day she's whining because you're not working; the next day, if you get a great job, she's whining because you're going to leave her. Don't listen to her. And take the opportunity not to feel sorry for yourself. *Your* future is in *your* hands. Feel free to live *your* life.

He grimaces as if about to cry, then manages to turn his dismay into a giggle.

- That's easy to say, know-it-all, since I think I'm a Rebeucop!

- It's not that easy, Malik, make no mistake. Well, I've got to go to bed. You want to sleep here tonight?

- On the floor? On the landing? No, ma'am. I'm not homeless, thank you! I'm a world champion at *losing*! I'll just wish you a good night anyway.

- Good night, Malik...

I'd like to take him in my arms. To shake him. To whisper the right words that would help him react before it's too late. I don't dare. I don't know. I just watch him go, a little wobbly, surely very sad to feel imprisoned... and perhaps imprisoned in his sadness.

I try to persuade myself that some decisions can't be made for others. You have to make them on your own. With the support of loved ones, yes, but alone.

So I close the door and hope there's a benzodiazepine tablet left. I need to sleep.

24.

One morning, I have a revelation: once again, I'm fossilizing.

After more than six months on the job, I feel like I know my job as an island warden inside out. I've become part of a close-knit team, particularly with Édouard, Hakim and Luca. I've discovered the residents, the little gangs of young people and the shopkeepers of the twentieth arrondissement. I can say with complete objectivity that, at that time, I knew the borough better than I knew my own pocket. I'm convinced that "îlotage" is the best form of police training. It's where you learn how to gather intelligence; where you're called upon to maintain order and support the emergency police; and where you become aware of the diverse but mutually enriching bonds that can unite a population and the civil servants charged with protecting them, even if sometimes in spite of themselves.

Right now, I feel fine. Which, for me, means I've got to get moving. If I'm satisfied with what I've got, once I've stabilized, I'm afraid I'll rot on my feet. There's something of that in my relationship with my job, and perhaps with my life in general. As soon as I feel I'm getting into my comfort zone, I want to get out of it so I don't become numb. If I've crossed a threshold, why stay where I am and not try to move on to the next level? The only way to get the answer is to aim higher. Elsewhere. Otherwise. To dare to take on a new challenge.

The Groupement de Soutien aux Îlotiers (GSI) is recruiting. In the twentieth arrondissement, this corps is led by Captain Jeanne Balard. I've heard unanimous compliments about her, which is rare! Officially, the GSI has two functions:

- assist colleagues in difficulty during their interventions, and

- managing urban violence, from rodeos and riots to ambushes against police forces.

Hakim and Édouard follow me in this adventure. Our three applications are submitted for the 6 p.m. to 2 a.m. slot. That's the most exciting time for a police officer who likes action. At the time, it didn't occur to us that these hours were incompatible with a fulfilling social and personal life. The excitement of joining the force and the prospect of a constant adrenaline rush freed us from pragmatic considerations, however important.

When we learned that the three of us had been detained, we were overjoyed. Immediately afterwards, I get my tonfa clearance and don my full set of gear: on the right, gun and handcuffs; on the left, tonfa and gas.

For my first shift, I'm teamed up with Vince and Dodo, two colleagues with different profiles. The most stylish is undoubtedly Dodo, a tall, dark-haired man wearing

- nibbling his cheeks,

- round rimmed glasses,

- always rolled in the beak, and

- worn biker leather.

Vince is more direct and gives me the lowdown on my first shift:

- At GSI, you have to be on your toes. We're always competing with our colleagues. The BAC and Police secours try to steal our best deals. Since we're on the same radio frequency, there's a lot of poaching going on!

- Hold on," says Dodo, pointing to a BMW. This one's a rental, so we'll pass it on.

The driver and passenger must be in their twenties. We report the license plate to the exchange. After a few seconds, the answer: stolen vehicle. Dodo's flair has struck. We put on the two-tone and the blue. I'm jubilant. My first outing in my new job, no water leaks, no school trips. It's a real thrill!

As soon as its occupants know they've been spotted, the sedan accelerates and tries to outrun us. Given the configuration, its chances are minimal. Nevertheless, driving at breakneck speed in such a densely populated area, the fugitives could cause a fatal accident at any moment. Vince sticks to the car to let it know that its fate is sealed. Eventually, the vehicle realizes the obvious. It pulls over.

We dismount, weapon in hand, aware of the danger: if they're drug couriers, they could pull out a Kalashnikov and sweep us off our feet... or use their sedan to ram us.

- Cut the engine!

As our captain, he assumes the riskiest position, on the driver's side. Vince moves to the passenger side... and then something unexpected happens. I see my colleague start to tremble. He gives me a distressed look and drops his pistol. Dodo looks up, dumbfounded. Without trying to understand (and I'll never know the end of the story), I step between him and the passenger to allow him to pull himself together and retrieve his weapon.

- Are you going to cut your engine?

The driver seems to take pleasure in provoking us. He lets the *suspense* build for a few seconds, then resolves to turn the ignition key.

- It's all right, sir, take it easy," he said in a drawl. We haven't done anything, there's no need to get so excited...

- I want to see your papers and the vehicle papers," decrees Dodo, gun still in hand. Quickly, now. And no sudden moves, understand?

- What's going on, sir? Seriously, that's abusive! We're peaceful, and you...

- The papers, cuts Dodo. Quickly, quickly.

The driver takes the elements provided by his passenger and hands them to my sidekick. He takes one look and realizes the mistake. In the guise of big-time smugglers, we've arrested two little idiots who "didn't have time to return the rental car" to the agency.

With that out of the way, I climb back into our vehicle to let Dodo explain to Vince about his discomfort. When they join me, Dodo says:

- You rocked it, Nora.

I'm shivering inside.

We've hardly left the house when we learn that there's been a disturbance in the Rue Joseph Python area. We're not far away, so we head over. Chic, no time to get bored!

Alas, not unhappy with their coup, the BAC sector beat us to it. They look great, with their gleaming uniforms and visible biscottos, surrounding their charismatic Captain Lorenzo. We, in our sneakers and caps, don't look like much... although I'm not sure we're any less effective. Clothes don't always make the policeman!

Acknowledging our defeat, we greeted our colleagues and took part in the control. When the police arrived, half a dozen individuals were smoking pot and drinking whisky under the windows of local residents who were annoyed by their loud voices. Anxious to do my part, I took one of the offenders in hand for a security check. The individual takes the opportunity to whisper insults in Arabic to me:

- You white trash whore... You're betraying the family... Aren't you ashamed, you slut?

After trying to ignore him, I explode and grab him by the collar, hissing:

- Will you shut your filthy mouth?

- What's going on, Nora?" asks Dodo.

- He insults me in Arabic. I can't take it.

My sidekick takes out his tonfa.

- I'd advise you not to go on like this, you little prick. We're not your buddies, you got that?

- We'll meet again, bitch," my admirer whispers.

His prescience was confirmed. Three quarters of an hour later, we're back with the BAC on rue Joseph Python: the offenders have resumed their untimely revelry. Courageous, these young people prefer to focus their invective and spitting on me. I intervene vigorously and, with my colleagues, we take five of them back to SARIJ. As I pass a mirror, I retch: my jacket is studded with molluscs. Disgusted, I have to wash it immediately, as the administration only provides us with one, and I can't stay in this state!

Here I am, dreaming of perpetual action, doing laundry. Luckily, my colleagues sense that I'm irritated enough not to want to hear any so-called manly jokes about a woman's normal role, which is, as everyone knows, to clean the laundry and not to be out in the field. I'm starting to think about tomorrow, so I don't need as much heat. My mother has invited me to lunch. I'm happy to see my parents again, but I'm wary. Tensions can flare up so quickly for no logical reason...

The next day, I realize that I was wrong to worry. My mother had prepared a sublime *mloukhya* - a kind of stew made from corte powder. Of course, in the Lakheal household, nothing is free. In the secrecy of her kitchen, my mother gets me a check so that my poor father can return to Tunisia. Aren't I rich, now that I'm a civil servant? At least this contribution saves me the trouble of making snide remarks and asking deliberately unpleasant questions. And then, after dinner, while my mother finishes gathering up the dishes, I have the opportunity to exchange a few words with my silent father... who even asks me a question, a rare event!

- How are the police?

- I'm fine.

- You're in the twentieth arrondissement, right? I remember building sites in Ménilmontant... It was 1975... I loved this neighborhood. There were Jews and Arabs there, we all mixed together... I spent whole evenings playing *chkoba* with Guy and Ayed... Well, that was before, what do you expect?

- Yes, things have changed quite a bit. Yesterday, an Arab I was controlling even insulted me, saying I'd betrayed him!

(I don't think it's necessary to mention all the other names I've been called. My father's no fool, he guessed them, but he wouldn't be happy to have his intuition confirmed).

- My daughter," he continues, "what do you think? Just because someone's Arab doesn't mean they're smarter than everyone else, unfortunately! Some Arabs think they're above the law. So they say that if a white man controls them, he's a racist; and you, because you're an Arab like them, they think you'll leave them alone. When they realize that you won't, what do you expect them to invent? They're left with insults. Let them bark, they're nothing. And now, go see your mother, *Derrick's* about to start.

Yes, I was wrong to be wary of this invigorating meal. Even against a "solidarity" cheque, a *mloukhya* and the words of a wise chibani: what better way to regain a certain serenity?

25.

In the months that followed, I remember bits and pieces.

The discovery of friendly, motivated colleagues.

Our hazing by the Ancients putting Vicks on the handles of our vehicle as we prepare to go out on patrol.

The encouragement of my great boss, Jeanne Balard, after a clean intervention.

My concern is not to be satisfied with what I have acquired. During my first year at the GSI, I was offered the opportunity to prepare for the qualification of Judicial Police Officer. Becoming an officer would open up new prospects for me, as it would allow me to draw up documents during legal proceedings, such as notification of police custody. More than just entitling me to the mini-premium that goes with this responsibility, "having the OPJ block", in the usual terms, would eventually enable me to apply to departments where such a qualification is required - the Judicial Police, for example. But it also requires unfailing motivation, because the preparation takes five months - and that's a long time!

During this period, we were seconded on a part-time basis to a training center in the Paris region, where we attended highly specialized courses, particularly in the legal field, which we then had to swallow by heart. I was lucky enough to find myself in a group that quickly bonded, helped and supported each other, until they achieved an exceptional statistic: we all qualified. As a result, I remember my individual and collective joy… and, in keeping with my admittedly rather special mentality, I remember the question that accompanied it: now what challenge will I take up?

I also remember an ambush in the Patrice de la Tour du Pin housing estate. We were called there to put an end to some noise pollution. When we got there, we couldn't hear a thing. We parked at the entrance to the estate and decided to check it out on foot. We don't notice any nuisance. Just as we were about to return to our car, fifteen youths armed with *baseball* bats and iron bars came towards us. I'm not proud of it at the time. First flabbergasted by this strange sight, I call for reinforcements and draw my gas and then my tonfa. Three against fifteen, our chances of long-term survival are slim. Fortunately, our colleagues from the BAC, led by the handsome Lorenzo, get us out of trouble before the situation really turns sour.

I remember that, even after that bout of heat, I obviously didn't regret choosing to be exposed to danger on every outing. Quite the opposite, in fact. I feel the reality of my new profession. I'm indignant at the unfathomable stupidity of human beings (attacking civil servants, and cowards at that, why on earth?). I'm learning to be more vigilant as soon as I leave the police station. And I feel I'm fulfilling myself by having to *challenge* and surpass myself every day.

As if to echo my conviction, the poet Patrice de la Tour du Pin, before being used as an incongruous name for a city, wrote, in "Au-delà de la joie":

> We must taunt all those who sink
> In the mediocre, in the flat,

All the weak, all those in the shadows,

Those who are not satisfied...[7]

Faced with the haters, the fools, the youngsters who imagine they have no more exciting activity to live up to than fomenting ambushes against peacekeepers, I won't settle for mediocre. I will not retreat. The more I'm challenged, the more opportunities I'll be given to forge ahead. The variety of missions entrusted to the GSI is a good illustration of this.

I haven't forgotten that poor twenty-something Ukrainian prostitute, cut in half by a speeding bus as she crossed a main street without looking. Nor have I forgotten the look on Edouard's face just as we were about to set off again, when he realized that he had forgotten the keys to our vehicle in the tarpaulin used as a temporary shroud for the deceased.

Fortunately, violence doesn't sum up my daily work life: I still remember the laughter I had in the break room with Hakim, Édouard and other colleagues.

However, my main memory of this period is of the first day of rest I took. It began with a fourteen-hour nap, which gives you an idea of how tired I was. When I woke up, I decided to treat myself to a good breakfast. I went down to the local bakery. It takes me a while to realize that there isn't a cat in the street. I ask the shopkeepers, who look at me with wide eyes.

- Haven't you seen the news?" they ask me, incredulous.

I confess I don't. They tell me to go home and turn on the TV. I comply... and discover that two airliners have crashed into the

---

7. Patrice de la Tour du Pin, *La Quête de la joie* [1939], Gallimard, "Poésie" [1967], 2002, p. 102.

World Trade Center. I can hardly believe it. As fascinated as I am horrified, I need to watch these unbearable images over and over again. As if, on the thousandth viewing, the planes were going to avoid the buildings, or someone was going to confess that it never happened...

Malik calls me, convinced that this massacre will boost racism against us.

- Since the Iraq war, we've symbolized absolute evil," he growls. Now, I'm not telling you...

I try to comfort him... even though I share his fears. Then again, I can't know what Bin Laden and his clique of bloodthirsty emirs have unleashed:

- the hard line of George Bush's hawks to justify their economic wars in the name of the Axis of Good;

- the spread throughout the West of this "Axis of Good" by euphoric racists; and

- the success of Muslim fundamentalists, taking advantage of my co-religionists' dismay at the rejection of some of their fellow citizens.

The change is brutal. I see it in the street and even, with certain colleagues, at work.

Before September 11, I was an Arab. Now I'm a Muslim. It gets worse.

At least you can spot an Arab. Muslims are more devious. They can come in any color and can count on two billion peers to enter your home, slit your throat and rape women and girls. So many analysts-experts-specialists strongly predict it...

This intuition was confirmed when I later studied how, little by little, "the other that overwhelms us has become Muslim".

Raphaël Logier has shown that the World Trade Center attacks boosted, first and foremost in the United States, "the idea that Europe was responsible for this disaster", since "for decades, it had been the stepping stone of Islamism and its gateway to the West"[8]. If all those who hate "the Muslims", as if they were a united bloc seeking to destroy "Judeo-Christian civilization", knew how difficult it is for us, within the same family, to organize a simple wedding, perhaps they would have a glimpse, reductive but significant, of the stupidity of their fears!

8. Raphaël Logier, *Le Mythe de l'islamisation. Essai sur une obsession collective*, Le Seuil [2012], "Points", 2016, p. 41.

26.

Over the weeks and months that followed, Søren Kierkegaard accompanied my dismay at this outpouring of more or less latent hatred and prejudice. The flashes of light in his *Diapsalmata* resonate with me, as when I read :

> My conception of life is completely absurd. I feel as if an evil spirit has placed on my nose a pair of glasses, one lens of which magnifies on an inordinate scale, while the other reduces on the same scale[9].

The more experience I gather, the more I realize how essential it is to fight against this natural tendency towards binary schematization. There aren't police torturers on one side, and young victims on the other; any more than there are good French people on one side, and bad Muslims on the other (or vice versa!). Ma vie illustrates the ambiguity that subsumes any clear-cut black-and-white judgment.

For example, I'm lucky enough to have a job I'm passionate about BUT I'm afraid I'll go soft as soon as I start to feel good.

---

9. Søren Kierkegaard, *Or else... or else. Un fragment de vie* [1843], *in: Œuvres*, t. I, trans. Régis Boyer and Michel Forget, Gallimard, "La Pléïade", 2018, p. 27.

I'm lucky enough to have finally furnished my apartment, BUT I wish my parents had come to see it. I'm lucky enough to have a happy life BUT I know that, when I close the door on my home, I'm alone, etc. I'm not alone just in my home. And it's not just then that I'm alone: when the colleagues I like catch me reading a book while waiting for the next patrol, they make fun of me, pointing out our irrefragable differences.

- Hey, Édouard, look!" thunders Hakim. Nora is still reading Zorro Kikigratte.

I rectify mechanically:

- Søren Kierkegaard. But tell me, Hakim, I didn't know you were a half-cop!

- What do you mean, do?

- Well, you know, half-cops are those who can't read.

Hakim grabs his little belly and laughs:

- Not a chance. I'd rather be a double cop!

- So, you're Kikigarde the car, Nora? intervenes Édouard as he arrives to add his two cents.

- And Kikongarde on sight today?" continues Hakim.

A firm and definitive diagnosis is required:

- You're two big, fat morons. Tomorrow, I'll bring you back a *Voici*. Is that all right, or is it a bit complicated for you?

- It's a bit complicated," admits Édouard, "there's a lot of text.

- Yeah, he's right," agrees Hakim. Bring us a *Playboy* instead. That's always useful!

Just then, the radio puts us back into work mode. We learn that an individual behaving suspiciously is wandering the streets of rue de Bagnolet. Hakim grumbles:

- And yet another rotten mission for Bibi and his fricotins...

- It's heavy," agrees Edouard, taking his place behind the wheel. We're not Police secours.

Hakim turns to me:

- Hey, Nora! He say anything about that, Kikecarte-les-cuisses?

- Wait, let me check... Um, yes, it's right there, look... Sorry, I forgot you couldn't read. Well, it says: let that big idiot Hakim go and see if I'm there.

- So let's go together!

We soon arrive on the scene and quickly regain our seriousness. Indeed, we spot a tall black man hopping along at a leisurely pace. He reminds me of a cosmonaut frolicking on the Moon.

- Leave me alone! he intimates as we approach. I'm being transformed.

- And what do you turn into, sir?" asks Édouard.

- In eight!

- I beg your pardon?

- You'd better go," he advises my colleague. Right now, I'm in three, it's okay. But when I switch to eight, you're in big trouble. I'm going to kill you all!

- So," intervenes Hakim, "maybe it's better if you turn into a zero and go home?

Stunned, the man looks at him with wide eyes.

- In zero? he repeats. My poor friend, you're crazy.

Then he bursts into sardonic laughter, shouting:

- I'm never going home! I'm going to become an eight!

- OK," concludes Hakim, "let's pinch him gently and take him to Tenon."

As Edouard grabs the man by the arm, I ask the strange man if he's taking any medication. Without listening to me, the man glares at Édouard and whispers:

- I wouldn't do that if I were you.

- Not what?

- Don't touch me. If you don't let go immediately, I'll turn into an eight, and then...

- I know, you're going to kill us. So, I'll cuff you up real quick, you get in the car and don't be a smartass, and you and we'll be fine. How's that?

The curious olibrius puts up no resistance, merely warning us that, when push comes to shove, we'll have it coming. Hakim tells dispatch that we're on our way to the IPP, the Police Psychiatric Infirmary.

I'm about to slam my car door when I spot Moussa. I get out of the car immediately. I don't believe it. The little delinquent we knew has mutated 100%. He wears a beard and a keffiyeh. I hail him:

- Hey, Moussa, what happened to you? Did someone put a spell on you?

- It's not nice to make fun, ma'am.

- I'm not making fun, I'm just surprised... Have you become religious?

- I found my way. I messed up too much. I took your advice. I've settled down. May Allah forgive me!

- Yes, well, I never advised you to...

- This is my way, madame. May Allah the Merciful ease your path to Him!

I'm left flabbergasted. Edouard pulls me out of my stupor by suggesting that I get back in the car as quickly as possible. Hakim has decided to play along with our questioner, and the show is not to be missed.

- So, what do you have to say to me, mon *vier*?" says the crew's Marseillais to our prisoner, as I return to the cabin.

- I tell you, I don't believe you.

- Don't you believe me? Of course you believe me! Your maximum is eight. When I want to, I go twelve. TWELVE! Can you believe it? What do you have to say to that, Mr. Eight?

The guy asks Édouard:

- Is it true that it's becoming twelve?

- You already know too much," replies my colleague in a sepulchral voice.

- I don't care. When I'm eight, I'll kill you. And you won't be able to transform, because you'll be dead.

- Not a chance, *old man*! I'll be twelve before you're eight. Well, we're in a hurry. So I'll tell you what: do you want me to become twelve right away, just to show you?

- Nah, tell him not to do that, man! begs Edouard. Not twelve! Not twelve!

- Shut up, it's not up to you.

- Eleven, at the most," insists Edouard. But not TWELVE!

- Stop it, it's our guest's choice. If he says yes, I'll do it.

- Say no, say no!" intervenes Edouard.

- Don't influence!

- I don't influence, I protect.

- Because," insists Hakim, "I have no problem reaching twelve. Of course, around here, you're going to enjoy it, but that's not my fault.

- Le onze et d'mi, s'il faut, pas-le-douze!

Robocop

- Dude, for the last time, you want to see what a twelve is?

- Well... no, put like that, I'd rather not.

- So behave yourself during the trip. Otherwise... PAN! I BECOME TWELVE!

The man is startled.

As Edouard hilariously starts off, Numéro Huit turns to me, half-panicked and half bewildered. With a pout, I reassure him and whisper:

- You don't have to worry. We're among madmen, so you'll be safe!

<h1 style="text-align:center">27.</h1>

Contrary to what Hakim, Édouard and I believed, the life of a GSI agent often resembles that of a Police secours agent. I like action and the unexpected; I've got it covered.

One day, Hakim and I are called to Buzenval for a family dispute. The captain accompanies us. I knock on the door and announce:

- Police! Open the door!

Footsteps. A man in boxer shorts and T-shirt opens the door. Small detail: he's carrying an impressive sword. Fashion of the moment, I guess...

Hakim draws his Manhurin. I reach for my tonfa. Our captain sighs and pulls out her weapon: a pack of Marlboros.

- Come on, put down your saber, let's have a smoke and have a quiet chat about what's going on, shall we?

Flabbergasted, the man lowers his saber and places it beside him. He reaches out and grabs the cigarette offered to him by the captain. We enter the apartment. Hakim retrieves the weapon. I stand between the man, his wife and their three-month-old child. I speak to the frightened young woman. She explains that she would like to leave her husband. He threatens to "chastise" her if she dares, and promises that once he's taken care of her, he'll commit hara-kiri.

Unsurprisingly, despite the drama of the situation, the victim refuses to press charges. With no further illusions, I leave her the SARIJ number, promise her that an OPJ will always be ready to listen, then we take the husband away.

At SARIJ, we hand over the individual to our colleagues. Then we drop off the captain, who has another emergency to attend to, pick up Dodo and set off again to patrol the streets of the twentieth arrondissement. I spot two small silhouettes hanging around, and then I get a *flash*. I hold my breath for a few minutes, then crack and announce to my partners:

- Here's something that's not done.

- Naughty!" laughs Edouard behind the wheel. You'll finally admit that you're hopelessly attracted to me, even on duty...

I ignore him - the most effective strategy with this inveterate joker - and go straight to Dodo:

- I've spotted some minors hanging around the neighborhood. It's 11:30 now. I think it's a good idea to take them home.

- Do you know them? Where do they live?

- No idea.

Dodo scratches the paws eating his cheeks and delivers his verdict:

- Well, there are three ways of looking at it. One, I'm not that interested in it, I'm not at GSI to be a cab for kids. Two, it's not in our remit. But, three, we've got nothing on fire. So, if there aren't any blackbirds, we can always keep an eye on the thrushes...

On Rue Bidassoa, we spot my targets. As soon as they see us, the kids take off. Dodo and I leap out of the car. After a mad sprint (they're fast, those kids!), we manage to catch them before anything dramatic happens. I tell them off:

- Goddamn it, going to the courtyard is bad manners, especially when you've got nothing to be ashamed of!

- We were scared," explains the tallest, panting.

- But that's stupid! The police are here to protect you!

- Where do you live?" asks Dodo.

- Montreuil.

- It's a long way from here! What do you make around here?

- Well, let's get busy...

- We'll take you back," decides our chef du soir, glowering at the local *drug dealers.*

Indeed, the street dealers have come closer together. They don't miss a beat of our exchanges. Dodo is right to be on his guard. It doesn't take long for a projectile to land on a vehicle that's disrupting the narcotics *business,* especially if it's a police car!

- What's your little name?" asks Dodo.

- I'm Yapo and he's Kouame.

- So get in our Porsche, Yapo and Kouame. The party's over for tonight!

The kids give us their address. When we arrived in the area, we found not so much a building as a dilapidated squat. Here too, we're on our guard. The topography, the half-light and the off-center nature of the place are all assets for the little punks who would like to take us on. We enter the building cautiously. Just as we reach the third floor, a shadow appears in a doorway. The children shout:

- Mommy!

An African woman in her forties is opening her door. She stands still as if the sky had fallen on her head.

- My darlings!" she exclaims. How stupid have you been again?

- None," Dodo reassures her. On the other hand, they're out on the twentieth, past midnight. I don't think this is a good idea. The place isn't very busy at this hour. It's dangerous for kids on their own. Do you realize that?

The lady nods and invites us in. The apartment is more than insalubrious. It's a tiny two-room slum. In the living room, a mattress serves as a sofa and bed for the children. The mother sleeps in another room, eaten away by mold. I get the impression that the management company that rents out these apartments is simply waiting for the building and its inhabitants to rot away. How can people be housed in such disgraceful conditions?

Yapo and Kouame's mother explains that she is hired for three hours of cleaning at La Défense in the morning, and three hours in the evening, when the office workers have gone home. She can't afford to pay someone to look after her monsters. We simply remind her of her duties as a parent, a tone below, and encourage her to contact her local social services as a matter of urgency, so that they can help her come up with solutions.

As we leave, my heart sinks as I think of the family we're leaving behind. Life has thrown her into a terrible situation, despite her efforts to preserve her dignity and that of her children. And I'm revolted when I think of the idiots who equate African mothers with unworthy egg-laying hens in a hurry to have eight children "so they can fuck France" and "collect the benefits". I know of few family tragedies directly linked to immigration; I know of many due to the shameless exploitation of the willing working poor.

28.

On our return, the BAC offers us a nightcap. Alcohol-free, of course, since we're on duty. Although I'm not crazy about Coke, this little party interests me because I'd like to change my specialty. I mention it to Dodo. Perhaps my profile might interest them? There are no girls in the plainclothes squad. But for the police, having an agent who's not afraid of the dark could prove useful...

Dodo is skeptical about their boss's reaction. However, he urges me to take a whiff of the atmosphere.

- It doesn't eat bread, does it? he sums up.

I was only waiting for this moderate encouragement to rush into the meeting room.

The guys are friendly, delighted I've come and funny in their own tonic way. When the unit's *big boss* deigns to speak to me, my optimism takes a beating.

- So, are you having a good time at GSI?" says the officer, more than a little condescending.

- It's a fascinating job, but I know that, in the police, you have to challenge yourself often to avoid falling into a rut...

- You're not wrong.

- Do you have any recruitment plans?

The colossus bursts out laughing loudly. He really seems to find my question hilarious.

- You're straightforward, but, you see," he finally bellows when he's calmed down, "as long as I'm alive, no nenette will fit into my unit.

- Well... why?

- You chicks are afraid of everything and you're a pain in the ass.

- I beg your pardon?

- Look at you! You're a hottie, so you'll be sleeping with half my boys. The other half will have it bad. As a result, I'm going to have a shitty atmosphere and, when it comes to going to the cardboard box, there'll be no solidarity, no group, no one. All because of a nenette that, the rest of the time, is useless to us. So, no, you'll never be one of us, Nora. Not even in dreams. You played it rough, I'd rather be clear with you.

I'm not so much disappointed as furious. I've seen a few racists and misogynists in the police force; I've seen fewer idiots as stupid. That notwithstanding, if this moron hopes to make me despair, he's got it all wrong. His contemptuous outburst has the opposite effect on me. Opposition stimulates me. While the police, as an institution, have always placed their trust in me objectively and attentively, some idiots in their ranks have stuck to an outdated mantra: a good policeman is white and male.

I devote all my professional energy to proving them wrong. Inwardly, when I confront their clichés, first it disgusts me, then it *boosts* me. I think of my beloved Søren Kierkegaard, and the passage in which he seeks to define "what is edifying in the thought that, vis-à-vis God, we are always wrong". He concludes:

> You may have wanted something many times, tried
> it out. However, it is only the deep inner movement,

the indescribable emotion of the heart that assures you that what you have recognized belongs to you, without any power being able to take it away from you; for only the truth that edifies is truth for you.[10]

Like Kierkegaard, I'm going to continue to build my truth by pursuing my "deep inner movement", the one that pushes me to go further, higher and stronger, if only to give fools and especially misogynist racists something to giggle at. But if, to encourage me, fate had the good idea of giving me a little push now and then, it wouldn't be a bad thing!

In the absence of a metaphysical sign, I concentrate on my work. I'm convinced that, sooner or later, my willpower and seriousness will pay off. So, the very next day, I'm back at it again. Just as I'm enjoying my *pasta alla* Daft Punk break (spaghetti in tomato sauce, with basil and onions, the recipe for which appears in the "Revolution 909" video), an alert mobilizes us. I jump into our vehicle. Tonight, I'm a sandbagger. In other words, positioned behind the driver, I'm in charge of his safety in case we pick up anyone who wants to attack him during his transfer.

Dodo is in charge and Édouard is driving. We leave in four vehicles, as a big rodeo is in progress. The uniformed BACs are called in to lend us a hand. Unlike my colleagues, I'm delighted about this, even if they sometimes steal the show when it comes to a good deal, because the main thing remains: the guys who make up the section are efficient and, above all, hyperbeautiful,

---

10. Søren Kierkegaard, *Or else... or else. Un fragment de vie* [1843], *in: Œuvres*, t. I, *op. cit.* pp. 770-778.

Robocop

hypermuscled, in short, hyperpleasant to look at - an innocent but not negligible pleasure...

By the time six of us arrive on the scene, the scooters have vanished into thin air. Either our two-tons have scared them off; or the offenders never existed, and we've been asked by the megaphone of tricksters to divert our attention from other areas. As if in obedience to the cop from "Revolution 909" repeating: "Stop the music and go home", we switched off our two-tone and were about to return to the police station when a BAC section chief called out to me:

- Is that you, Nora?

I nod. He invites me to join him, a little way from the other officials.

- We've been watching you for a while, along with your colleagues, and the opinions are unanimous: you're doing pretty well...

I say thank you, looking a little indifferent to mask my excitement. After the snub I got the other night, is some hustler going to come and poach me personally and offer me a place in his unit? It would be a nice way of thumbing my nose at the head of the night BAC!

- I've been told that the intelligence service is looking for a colleague of North African origin who's got it in the britches," continues the poet. Would that tempt you?

- Well... yes, why not, when do we start?" I say, trying to imagine what could have led someone to think that I had something in common with James Bond.

- Tomorrow, I'll give you the number of the commander who's recruiting. On the other hand, you're not to mention this to anyone, understand? I just congratulated you on your behavior in the field.

And with that, the officer turns on his heel.

- Are you moving, Nora?

I join them in time to enjoy Edouard's joke.

- That's the problem with chicks," he sighs. They're always the last ones in the car...

It would have been a shame to miss his new wit! Knowing him as I do, I don't react to my colleague and friend's provocation. For the moment, I'm stunned and exhilarated by the unexpected joy I feel. Two mysterious letters flash behind my eyelids: RG, RG, RG... Will I be up to this next challenge: joining the most mysterious department in the whole national police force? Absurd question. You have to, SO I will.

29.

My enthusiasm fizzled out.

As soon as I get home, I have doubts. I tell myself that the BAC major only came to see me to make a pass at me. As he's not the *sexiest* member of his *boy band*, he's found a lame excuse to approach me, and I, whether *desperate* or a sucker, have gone along with it. Even the next day, when, as agreed, I picked up the cell phone of a so-called recruiter, I had little faith in the reality of this "Commandant Thierry". Suspicious, I expect my contact to arrange a meeting in an ambiguous location. Then I'll finally be able to dispel this grotesque deception and move on.

Except that Commandant Thierry doesn't seem to be laughing in the slightest. He made an appointment for me to meet him at the Hôtel de Beauvau, two days later. An unambiguous location, the heart of the Ministry of the Interior.

I have no choice but to study for my interview. But what do I have to study for? I try to find out something about the Renseignements généraux. What I find is vague. There's nothing solid about the knowledge I'm accumulating.

I'm exploring another avenue: I'm trying to gather my knowledge of Islam. Although I believe in Allah, I don't know much about my religion in depth. My parents didn't raise me *in* Islam. They are not practising Muslims. Like many chibanis, my father gave up religion to assimilate and, to his great advantage, drink red wine. My mother also took the opportunity to give up her religion: in her opinion, "living near an alcoholic" haramized her living space, making it impossible for her to practice her religion. Everyone finds a red herring wherever it suits them!

In short, of Islam, I know what the school taught me, *id sunt* the five pillars:

- the shahada (profession of faith),
- prayer,
- the month-long fast for Ramadan,
- zakât (alms to be offered), and
- the pilgrimage to Mecca.

In my bag, I also have a few suras I learned one summer in Tunisia, when I was bored. They remain vivid in my memory, as I continue to recite them when I feel the need to pray.

In realizing my ignorance, I'm not yet aware of the extent of the damage that can result from situations like the one I experienced. Many young people of my generation, noting the rejection of them by part of the French population, will blame their parents for not having raised them in the Muslim faith, which would have given them less of a substitute identity. Not considered French, they can't even call themselves Muslims. This reality would later have two extremely perilous consequences for the nation.

- On the one hand, the arrival of the Wahhabis, who opposed the absence of religion with a rigorist version of Islam, conducive to all kinds of obscurantist excesses and recruitment.

- On the other hand, the boom in school drop-out rates, with new churchgoers - our very own *reborns*! - are quick to send their children to Salafist or home schools, rather than to the institutions of the Republic.

This point is essential. For me, today as in the past, the veil in the public space is not dangerous. The most important thing is to find a way of reconnecting with the children of the Republic, for it is they who have been lost more than the territories.

At the time I applied to join the RG, Salafism was expanding, but not yet on the scale it had become in France. Nonetheless, as early as 2001, a misunderstanding of the phenomenon began to emerge. Most of the specialists who were quick to strut their stuff on television in the wake of the New York attacks were merely opportunists with a lot of nerve and self-importance. And this trickery is neither specific to the 2000s, nor exclusive to current events. Every dramatic event has its share of vocations.

In the wake of the *Charlie Hebdo* and Hyper-Casher attacks, for example, a journalist who, the day before, was unrivalled in advising women on how to reduce their cellulite, has now discovered a new and more profitable specialty: secularism. Others take advantage of their fear of Islam by systematically confusing the religion with Salafism. In this vein are

- political *losers*, for whom the fight against Islam represents a new chance to exist;

- recent French arrivals who want to settle their accounts with the religion of their country of origin... while disregarding, in the process, *our* history, i.e. the history of the Maghreb community in France, as distinct from their experience abroad.

We are fortunate to live in a democracy, under the 1905 law, which allows every citizen to practice his or her religion in complete peace of mind, as long as public health and safety are not compromised.

In April 2002, when I prepare for my interview at the Place Beauvau, I'm not likely to come across as an expert. I don't have the nerve. I can barely recite the *fatiha*, the first sura of the Koran, which praises Allah and asks him to guide us along the path of those he has blessed with his favors. However, I doubt that a job interview at the RG would ask you to recite the Koran! I hope they won't test my practical knowledge either, as I'm not religious.

Suffice it to say that, armed with my etic religious knowledge and my ignorance of the RG, I'm in a bit of a bind as I head off to 11, rue des Saussaies to take the interview of my life and become the first woman to join the Renseignements Généraux' anti-terrorist unit specializing in Islam. The nec plus ultra. The holy of holies.

Nora, my good girl, there's nothing left to do.

30.

Through the airlock, a man named Zied comes to pick me up. He's in his thirties. I notice he's wearing a white Lacoste suit and *jeans* far too big for him. He takes me three floors up, *through* secure corridors, to Commander Thierry. I'm struck by the nickelitude - I'll try the neologism - of the premises. Everything is clean and functional. It's a far cry from the dilapidated twentieth-century police station, and a far cry from the smell of urine emanating from the cells where detainees languish in police custody!

The captain is waiting for me behind his desk. Disappointingly for the midget in me, it's not Sean Connery, Pierce Brosnan or Daniel Craig. Rather, it's a small, self-effacing, bent forty-something, whose face instantly marks his interlocutors: hard features and piercing blue eyes. The kind of person you don't even wonder if he's ever laughed at a good old-fashioned rotten joke with a bottle of beer in his hand.

The boss invites me to sit down and attacks me head-on:

- So, I hear you do well in complicated environments. I understand you're not afraid of the inner cities and tough neighborhoods. What can you tell me about that?

- I've been working in the neighborhoods for three years. My group reinforces colleagues in difficulty and tries to pacify the tensions that can arise. I try to make my contribution as best I can.

- Do you practice combat sports?

- I've been doing French boxing for the last five years, both in clubs and in police structures. What's more, whenever the opportunity arises, I sign up for all the training courses that enable me to perfect my skills in dealing with difficult stops.

- We've seen that in your file, which is a positive point. Here, we specialize in the fight against Islamist terrorism. What do you think of Islam in France today?

I take a deep breath before answering the question I've been dreading.

- Commander, I deplore the September 11th attacks, as I'm sure the vast majority of French people do. However, deploring does not exempt us from taking action. As a police officer, I want to help prevent all kinds of attacks on our territory. If I join your department, I'll be able to do this day and night.

- What do you know about our service?

I smile and say:

- I know it's very secretive. So secretive that it's almost impossible to get reliable information about what's going on there.

- Just so you know, in the world of intelligence, SORS, the specialized operational and research section, is the elite of tailing.

- If you think I'm worthy, I'd be honored, I admit.

- Do you know any colleagues at the Direction de la Surveillance du Territoire?

- No.

- Good news. Our agents don't have to rub shoulders.

- I'll remember that.

- You're here for a reason: we're a group of men. Current events force us to evolve. Our authorities have strongly advised us to recruit *a* female agent. Let me be clear: I comply with this injunction without enthusiasm. So, at the first incongruity, such as an affair of the heart or an affair of the buttocks likely to disrupt the existing team, the adventure will end immediately. Have I made myself clear?

I nod in agreement. Now's not the time to tell you that I've recently heard the stupid equation "woman = ass story" and that, even in premises far more chic than a meeting room in a local police station, it makes my skin crawl. I'll have my revenge. If I'm chosen, I'll prove that I belong where I'm needed, if not welcome. It'll be the best way of slapping the doughnut out of those idiots blinded by their fantasies and stereotypes.

- It also works for your life in general," insists the commander. If you join this service, you commit to me that you won't get pregnant for three years. Any objections?

- No, it wasn't in my plans.

- Very good. Do you speak Arabic?

- Tunisian Arabic, yes.

- Question?

- No, sir.

- You're dismissed. For your information, there are seven candidates. You will receive an answer in the next few days. Zied will show you out.

I leave and return to my quarters, ranting and raving. I thought I was a loser, and I'm angry with myself for being reasonable enough not to be openly annoyed by the commander's unabashed machismo. But then I think, maybe this was a test of my ability to keep my nerve. At this level of responsibility, a commander can't be as stubborn as this one has endeavored to appear. Who knows if my ability to absorb his misogyny with the phlegm of habit (that's also what "being a philosopher" is all about!) won't make the difference with my competitors?

From then on, I was hopeful. I wasn't brilliant during the interview, that's fine. But

- I've got a university education that others probably don't have, which sometimes gives me a little extra ability to think... and may make it easier to write those white notes for the hierarchy;

- I have field experience and a spotless track record;

- During my young career, I have demonstrated my desire to progress and my ability to adapt;

- I proved I could keep my cool in tense situations;

- I know how to manage a team;

- I can take the initiative;

- I'm sporty and

- I'm an Arabic speaker.

What's up?

So I wait. I oscillate between the rage of having missed the opportunity of a lifetime and the hope that my past professional life will have spoken for me. Every passing second is double-edged. On the one hand, since they don't call me back, I deduce that they don't want me. On the other hand, as long as they haven't said no, I deduce that they're thinking about it, which means I've got a chance.

Worried and disturbed, I let myself see signs everywhere. I become superstitious as hell... without totally abandoning my lucidity. I think of the image used by my dear Søren Kierkegaard.

> What philosophers say about reality is often as specious as when, in a junk shop, you read on a sign: "Ici, on repasse" ("Here, we iron"). If you brought your laundry in to be ironed, you'd be fooled, because it's only the sign that's for sale.[11]

The "signs" are so many signs that fool me. In metaphorical terms, I'd say I spend my time taking my laundry to the junk shop. When I think I hear my phone vibrate, I know I'm spoken for... but there's no text, I've been dreaming. Since I'm not being contacted, I know I've been eliminated. But I still want to believe it; and, at the same time, if I tell myself it's possible, I'll get the evil eye. Argh! The only advantage of this *suspense is* that it keeps my mind occupied... until the verdict is in.

This time, there's no room for doubt.

I'll have to abandon my family in the twentieth.

Dodo, Édouard, Vince, Hakim, we won't be working together anymore.

I'm so saddened by this that I can't understand why all my colleagues congratulate me and even ask me to contact them if, by chance, there's a vacancy in my future department.

I'm off to Renseignements Généraux, a prestigious department where I'll be the first woman to work. It's the perfect challenge for me, and a fresh start that some would consider a career achievement. Without raising my voice (I explain the above to show how out of touch I am with reality), I should be the happiest of policewomen. Nevertheless, at my farewell party, forgetting the

---

11. Søren Kierkegaard, *Or else... or else. Un fragment de vie* [1843], *in: Œuvres*, t. I, *op. cit.* p. 36.

exceptional opportunity I've been offered and that I've managed to land, I shed my tearful eyes at the thought that I'm leaving my friends - real friends: eighteen years later, we're still meeting up to feast together... I think my psychoanalyst can rest assured: she and I still have work to do!

THIRD PART

THE CHAMELEON

31.

This Saturday is the big day! I've been inducted into the Renseignements Généraux. I can hardly believe it, and the morning feels like a dream. Commandant Thierry introduces me to my peers in the Islam group:

- Jean-Baptiste is the biker - I immediately notice his muscular colossus stature;

- Jérémie and Stéphane take care of the car;

- Alexandre, Mehdi, Khaled and Yacouba are in charge of the pedestrian line; and

- Michel is our regular technician.

The boss gives me my first instructions:

- You're no longer in uniform. Subsequently, don't forget to carry your requisition card and armband with you at all times, whatever your outfit. The aim is to take them out as little as possible, because discretion is our watchword. We have to go unnoticed. No jumping up and down. I insist: we're not here to question. We're observers. We're here to find out, discover, understand and explore. Your best uniform, therefore, is a discreet outfit in which you feel comfortable. No jewelry, no heels. The simplest, least conspicuous clothes imaginable.

- Noted.

- On Monday, you'll receive all your equipment. Today, we'll give you your discrete, and then you'll be free to go and buy the outfit you need to enter the mosques.

End of *briefing*.

Michel hands me my "discret", an almost invisible earpiece connected to a transceiver. I can't wait to wear it and hear it sizzle!

Formalities out of the way, I head back to my neighborhood with one question on my mind: what does a woman-who-goes-to-the-mosque wear? I haven't been there very often, and I have the impression that there are as many obediences as there are mosques! Intuitively, I imagine that a practicing woman wears a hijab, doesn't wear make-up and invokes God at every turn. I'm going to have to deconstruct my clichés and clarify my vision of "the good Muslim woman" according to the criteria of the potentially most problematic religious figures: the Salafists.

That's why Barbès is *the place to be*. The advantage: I'm like a fish in water here, even if the neighborhood has changed since the 1980s! The tired bars where old Kabyles used to stagnate in the fumes of Jack Daniel's are gradually disappearing, replaced by shops selling books and religious accessories. The attacks of September 11, 2001 accelerated this transformation, stimulating the proselytizing of rigorists often financed by Saudi Arabia. By chance, I enter one of these now typical stores, with their green and white storefronts topped by a calligraphic sign.

- May Allah's peace, mercy and blessing be upon you, sister!" the shopkeeper says in Arabic, without looking up.

Stunned by the solemnity of the greeting, I jump straight to the reason for my visit:

- I'm looking for a djellaba and a veil to go to the mosque, but I'm not really used to...

Suddenly, the man deigns to look at me. His eyes sparkle with emotion. He suspects that I want to leave my sinful path and return to the religion of our fathers. Perhaps, for him, I'll be the source of a *hassanat,* those good deeds towards God that a believer must accumulate if he hopes to receive his reward in heaven. And to contribute to the conversion of an unbeliever is the ultimate hassanat!

- That's fine, sister," he replies gravely. I'll show you what I have in stock. What size are you?

- 38.

He hands me a firecracker-green djellaba. I try not to laugh as I think of the commander's phrase earlier this morning: "Discretion is our watchword."

- I think I prefer the navy blue," I say.

- Excellent choice! For the veil, look, the fabrics are there. Take the one that suits you.

Uncomfortable, I look at the scarf bin. How do you put on and take off a hijab? Is there any particular way? I need something practical and quick. Practical, because if I show up badly dressed, I run the risk of betraying my status as a newcomer and being noticed. Quick, because if I take too long to take it off, I could compromise my safety.

My eyes scan the store for a solution, and I come across some clutches marked "hidjab". I grab one and ask:

- Those are veils, too, aren't they?

- Yes, but they have the defects of their qualities. They're very quick to put on, because you just juxtapose these two ends, but I have to warn you: the fabric isn't great.

I'm blown away by the ingenuity and *marketing* savvy demonstrated by the Wahhabis. They should have thought of it, making a cheap *hijab kit* for lost souls wishing to reconnect with Islam without having to worry, so to speak!

The kit consists of a fabric to cover the head and another to cover the neck and shoulders. Just what I need. All sold for five euros. I take one black and one blue, then head for the books. I opt for the *bestseller* for neophytes, *Savoir faire la prière*, a *digest of* the ablutions and suras essential for praying.

The shopkeeper is on cloud nine. He encourages me to come back, offers me some incense to carry my prayer and escorts me off with the great Salafist phrase:

- May God make the path to him easier for you!

As soon as I go out, I rush home to try on my new outfit.

No irony here. Even if this shopping trip is for professional reasons, I've come to feel at home in this boutique; and as someone who, when the occasion calls for it, doesn't shy away from *sexy* cleavage, I finally have the opportunity to dress so-called like my ancestors and "see what it's like". Yes, I'm curious to see what a veiled Nora looks like, just as I was curious to find out what I looked like with my pistol at police school.

Especially as I've never worn a veil. In Tunisia, I saw veiled aunts and cousins. For me, it was a no-no. Hiding is out of the question. So I can't wait to see what I look like as a practicing Muslim! What's more, as with the Manhurin, I want to check if I'm credible with my new *dress code*. Miroir, my beautiful mirror, reassures me: my outfit makes me look really ugly, but it suits me just fine - that's the main thing. I'll be able to enter any mosque without a care in the world... and continue to attack my thought reflexes.

Indeed, I'm a little embarrassed by the idea of wearing a hijab. Like many French people, I tend to equate the veil with female submission and terrorism. I'm less excusable than my compatriots because, deep down, I *know*, though I forget, how ridiculous this belief is. My aunt Khadija is veiled, and I don't know many people who are as far removed from the ideology of the bombers as she is. As for being submissive... She's the one who bosses her husband around. Veil or no veil, the man better take it easy, I guarantee it!

Likewise, my cousins may be veiled, but they're not little nunnery saints who spend their time moping about. As soon as they hear I'm coming back home, they contact me to bring back make-up and, last but not least, handbags. They love going out dancing with us non-veiled girls. They veil because it's part of their religious practice, not because they live in an archaic world that needs to be debunked! And I, who spontaneously had this reductive reflex, am I not the proof of the absurdity of this amalgam demonizing the veil? If someone were to come across me in my Muslim garb in a small middle-class town, I can only imagine the reactions I'd provoke, ranging from commiseration to fear. But do I become dangerous because I wear the hijab? On the contrary, I'm adopting the codes that will enable me, in my own small way, to help save lives.

As I try on my work clothes, I realize how much is at stake and how complex the subject is. What do we really know about the veiled women we brush up against? By what shortcut of thought do we think we're free to reduce them, without distinction, to victims thrown helplessly under the thumb of smug obscurantists? Are Jewish women who wear wigs decerebrate? Are Catholic nuns intrinsically doomed to misfortune and enslavement? Did

Mother Teresa fail to make her own way? Obscurantism is independent of the hijab. It can exist with or without a piece of cloth. Otherwise, it would be easy to recognize it, whatever form it took!

To use a Hegelian distinction that Jean-Paul Sartre reinvested in *Being and Nothingness*, the veil has no meaning "in itself". It is only "for itself", that is, it takes on the meaning that each individual specifically attributes to it. According to the philosopher, it is even in this attribution of meaning that man's humanity nestles: man is thrown into the world without essence, and must construct an ontology for himself through his existence. This is why the metonymic reduction of a woman to her veil - as if she were no more *than* the veil she wears - and to what it means, not to her, but to us who see her, according to *our* imagination, is the source of a dramatic misunderstanding that corrodes social peace as soon as Islam comes into play.

Nevertheless, disregarding clichés and my own thoughtfulness, I complete my mutation by pondering my *kunya*, my rigorist practitioner nickname. I opt for Alya Oum Hakim. My parents come from the locality of Alya (which means "the one on high"), and I like the sound of the word. As for Hakim, it's not a nod to my dear Marseillais from the twentieth arrondissement police station, but a tribute to the convert nickname borne by Akhenaton, the singer of the IAM group I adore.

One last look in the mirror convinces me. That Saturday in April, in Barbès, from the chrysalis of Nora Lakheal escaped the butterfly Alya Oum Hakim, the future superheroine of the RG!

32.

Despite the commander's solemn welcome, despite the handing over of my "discret", despite the purchase of my perfect practicing Muslim disguise, I find it hard to believe that the new recruit to the group considered to be the elite of surveillance and shadowing, is me! It's hard to believe that, like and with her peers, Nora Lakheal is the last resort of local RG colleagues, when they feel that the case they've uncovered is too big for the technical and human resources at their disposal. It's hard to convince myself that I'm part of the team kept in reserve to deal with the most serious suspicions of terrorism (known as the "top end of the spectrum").

However, I am aware of our missions:

- monitor the activities of individuals suspected of planning attacks, particularly Islamist ones;

- determine their habits and draw up as complete a picture as possible of their environment;

- ensure the safety of colleagues, mainly the "techs" who are responsible for

    - to "soundproof" living spaces,

    - install cameras in strategic locations and

    - mark out interesting vehicles.

It requires daring, astuteness, intuition and long-term concentration. What's more, it requires motivation because, as we're warned from the outset, we can be away on a mission for long periods; we can be mobilized at any time; and we're bound to absolute silence, which doesn't help defuse tensions with boyfriends, partners or spouses!

The boldness and *tutti quanti*, I'll show it in the field. It's in the field that you show off your skills. In these areas, proof is everything.

On the other hand, I can vouch for my motivation. Because I've always given my all to prove myself worthy of the challenges offered to me. Because I wouldn't have been recruited if my file hadn't provided solid proof of my drive. And finally, because the individuals we're fighting against - often repeat offenders who, as soon as they're out of prison, aspire to plunge back into the preparation of new "actions", to use the well-known euphemism - represent a gangrene for my religion. I don't want to let these people stigmatize us and carry out attacks in France.

On Monday, I'm going to be introduced to the technical services. Zied takes me there, as proud as if he were honoring me with his own home!

It's Thomas who greets me in the vast basement work-shop-office, one of the best-protected areas in the department. Here again, the clichés fall away. Shaped by TV and film entertainment, I'd imagined an azimuth old man, like Emmett Brown, the "doc" from *Back to the Future*. I'd anticipated finding myself face to face with a crazy guy, capable of taking me by the arm to show me his latest invention, an invisible microphone capable of recording anyone's thoughts... but which would have exploded the moment he switched it on, re-doing his blow-dry and covering me in ashen dust.

Thomas is nothing like the Doc or Major Boothroyd, alias Q, from James Bond! He's a tall, blond-haired, blue-eyed man who's very composed, almost shy, yet instantly radiates his passion in the way that people who've found a profession that suits them like a glove often do. Little by little, I learn his story. Under pressure from his parents, he had to study to become a notary. Until the day he admitted he'd rather become a police officer. He passed the exam and was spotted by the RG during his year at school, where he demonstrated his talents as a tinkerer.

And so, exceptionally, he landed at Place Beauvau as soon as he was released. The recruiters were right on the money. This guy is even better than Angus MacGyver, and in real life! He knows how to slip his own miniaturized cameras into plants; he sets himself no technical limits; he spends his time, including his rest periods, imagining, manufacturing and testing new gadgets. One day, I'm sure, he'll manage to slip a camera into a hairpin... unless he's already accomplished that feat.

The first time we meet, he starts by checking my weapon and laughs when he spots my Manhurin.

- You'll have to go to the armory to get a Glock," he says. It'll be more practical.

My eyes sparkle. In my mind's eye, the Glock is Aymeric's and the other police *stars'* gun. It has an American action-movie feel, whereas my barrel pistol smacks of dusty westerns. The Glock is both prestigious and practical. It's lighter than a Manhurin, easier to handle, and can be loaded with fifteen rounds of ammunition, instead of six for my current pistol. BACs dream of this automatic, and I've been offered one!

Yet I know I'm not going to collect my Glock. I don't want to give up the gun I've been carrying for three and a half years. It took me a while to get used to it, but now we're inseparable. I love the way it looks - small, grey, shiny, elegantly curved. I refuse to part with her... until the institution forces me to. The year I join the RG, Sig Sauer ousts Manhurin from the national police market. Its SP 2022 gradually became compulsory. So I ended up having to return my first pistol. What I'm about to confess is ridiculous, but never mind: when we parted, I remember having tears in my eyes and giving her a big kiss. I'd trembled with her. I'd shown off with her. And, above all, we'd never shot anyone. She and I were made for each other, and we'd gotten along wonderfully.

- Wait a minute," says Thomas, "I haven't introduced you to the team that's here today. You must have heard the rumor that we're crazy, because we spend our lives in the basement, amongst ourselves, and no one understands our jokes. But it's not true! In reality, we're worse. For example, Vianney, the youngest of the bunch... Don't try to guess who he looks like: he's a cross between Harry Potter, because of his little glasses, and Dustin Diamond, the Screech from "Saved by the bell", because of his bush.

I couldn't agree more. It couldn't be better described!

- He has three specialities: he's an excellent pilot, even if that's of no use to us; he's the beacon specialist, which is more useful to us; and he's the computer king, capable of infecting any computer with a bug of his own making. He does have one flaw: he never has time. For anything. Except for programming. So you can make fun of him without worrying, he won't even turn his head towards you. In short, I have to admit it, although I'm not all that happy about it: Vianney is definitely 100% crazy. At his level of madness, there's nothing anyone can do for him. Too bad, we like him just the way he is, so let's keep him!

Turning to a thinning white-haired agent, Thomas continues:

- I'd also like you to meet Esteban. He's our grandpa, even if he doesn't like to be called that. His specialty? Locks. You show him a photo of a lock model, and he'll make you the corresponding key in a few hours. Well, unless his fishing went badly the day before, or his granddaughter nearly burned herself getting near the Sunday barbecue, but that's rare... Otherwise, he's incredible. In fact, I think he's crazy too. To have a gift like his, you have to be crazy. You see, on reflection, apart from me, of course, everyone here is crazy. Careful, now! You don't have to believe me, but don't kid yourself: you'll find out the hard way...

Seduced by my interviewee's energy, which shows his love of the profession and his admiration for his colleagues, I'm also struck by the contrast with what we're sold on TV. In the real world, spies are ordinary, undetectable people, surrounded by technicians with superhuman gifts, some of whom look like harmless retirees and others like typical thirty-somethings, somewhere between *geek* and classic BG. Thanks to our missions in the provinces, during which we sometimes spend long weeks together, I'll be able to discover the surprising personalities hidden behind the stubborn talent of the department's Géo Trouvetou.

- In any case, it's great to see some fresh blood on the team! exclaims Thomas. Plus, for once, they've found someone who looks normal, which makes a change.

I shrug:

- We can look normal compared to you!

- What do you mean, "compared to us"?

- You guys can do amazing things! Some nights, I find it hard to open my door with my key, so making a key just by knowing the captain's age...

- The photo of the lock, don't exaggerate, Esteban will blush.

- Age, photography... For all the difference it makes!

- Ha, Nora, Nora! Don't let yourself be impressed just because we know how to tinker. What you do when you're out and about is important and more dangerous, so it's at least as impressive. Get this into your head: the RG works on two legs, the technical and the human. If we don't give you a hand, you'll struggle; if you're not there, we're useless. Okay, enough chit-chat. I believe you were given your discrete the day before yesterday? This is a mini-recorder. When you go out on the trail, remember to take both with you.

- Tomorrow, we're offering you a mini-training session at the filoche in Paris," Zied informs me. You'll be able to try out the bazaar, which, by the way, is super-expensive. So, one, you take good care of it; and two, your first reflex, or almost your first reflex, when you leave here, will be to charge the battery as much as possible. It would be an exceptionally serious malpractice to run out of battery power because you've forgotten this.

Although I'm dying for it, I don't answer "Yes, Daddy" with a sigh. Promising myself to slap his doughnut with my next exploits, I simply say:

- Impeccable! I can't wait to take action.

- First, you'll stop at the range for your assignment shot. Yacouba is waiting for you there.

I thank Thomas and follow Zied towards the exit.

In the police force, the shooting test is compulsory when you change departments. I'm not particularly worried about it. Since school, I've often trained at the shooting range at Porte de la Chapelle. I've tamed my weapon. I've perfected my technique. But the eternal doubt lingers insidiously in the mind of the shooter (or Nora, or both): will I be up to the task? The risk of a bad session is never zero. A bit of fatigue, a lapse in concentration, a stray thought, the slightest touch of stress, and goodbye to the perfect score!

So I think that, when the worst is possible, the best is probable. So statistically, my first RG test should go well...

33.

The next day, I'm in high spirits.

The shooting session with Yacouba went wonderfully well.

Firstly, because I proved to my colleague that I'm just as precise and enduring as he is: after an hour's work, strong hand or weak hand, we finished *ex aequo*. At least in that respect, I proved that I wasn't there by chance! (Of course, you don't get into SORS by chance, but I'm sure I'll have to prove it by living up to the role I've been given!)

Secondly, because Yacouba, who didn't expect me to be at his level, gave me a new nickname, rather flattering in this context: Terminator.

Finally, because I have a hunch that Yak will become a friend. I like his humor, his restraint, his kindness.

Suffice it to say that I'm pumped up for my first pedestrian shadowing exercise, especially as I'm putting the pressure on myself. I keep repeating to myself that I'm on trial. I don't want to fail. First and foremost for myself, let's be honest! But also for my female colleagues who must be dying to join us. I don't want to hear the dreaded litany:

- No, we don't take girls anymore. We once recruited a girl from the twentieth arrondissement. On paper, she looked great, ticked all the boxes, and...

- And?

- Ben, given his performance, we decided to do without the girls.

I won't be the gravedigger of my sisters in uniform.

Wearing dark Gazelles, black *jeans*, an imitation leather jacket and a jet-colored scarf, my discreet earpiece, I wait for my companions at Nation station, on the RER side. My mission, since I've accepted it, is to follow Yacouba without him spotting me. Zied will be watching.

The starting gun is fired.

- From Zied to Nora, the lens train pulls into the station. I repeat: the objective train pulls into the station. The individual is in the middle carriage.

- Roger.

I position myself behind the other travellers, more towards the first third of the platform, to see where my target is. I catch a glimpse of Yak. Quickly, I go up to the next door to avoid being spotted. I'm obsessed with the principle: "Not too close to avoid being spotted, not too far away to avoid being unhooked." Yak is sitting by the door. I can smell a trick. From where he is, he can either go out when the doors close, and *ciao* Nora; or go out when the doors ring and come back in when they close, immediately spotting the chick who's imitating him... and hi, Nora!

I'm concentrating hard so as not to be fooled like the beginner I am. Ready for any eventuality, I stare at the back of Yak's neck during the critical start-up period. My senses are alert. My brain is firing on all cylinders. I understand why my colleagues warned me that shadowing is exhausting: even when nothing's happening, we're as tense as bows, even though we have to pretend to be ordinary bystanders!

For the moment, my colleague doesn't move an ear. I report the situation.

- From Nora to Zied, we leave the Gare de Lyon. The objective is still in the train, heading for Paris.

- Got it, Nora!

I breathe to relax, because I *know* what lies ahead. At the next station, we arrive at Châtelet-les-Halles. This is Europe's largest underground station. It handles almost thirty million passengers a year, brings together three RER trains sharing seven tracks on four platforms, is served by five metro lines and is linked to a huge shopping mall. In short, the place is either a perpetual anthill or one hell of a mess. No doubt about it: the test really begins here.

Bingo! When the train stops, Yacouba pretends to hesitate, then gets off. I imitate him, one door further on, not a little proud to have anticipated his little game. When the departure bell rings, Yak glances left and right, then up again. It was just a safety trick. Furious with myself, I barely have time to throw myself into the train as the doors close.

I warn Zied that we're off again, and try to squeeze in behind a traveler, as Yak is now facing my direction. The difficulty is twofold: I mustn't be noticed; and I still have to check on the sly what my lens is up to. At the next station, I have to glance behind me. My colleague remains tan in the train. It's at La Défense that he leaps out of the train and mingles with the crowd.

- From Nora to Zied, down to La Défense. I can still see him. He walks towards Courbevoie.

- Roger!

I see Yacouba take the big escalator to the exit. In front of me, a woman in a boubou carries her baby in her arms. I slip in behind her. Except that the child's bottle falls at my feet. I bend down to pick it up. The mother thanks me... and I see that Yacouba has disappeared. My first careless mistake and I was trapped. Nora's such a dullard!

In a panic, I reach the open air. I scan the esplanade from all sides. Nearby, a square. I go for it. No Yak in sight. Only alternative: a PMU on the square. If he's not there...

There he is, with Mehdi, sipping a coffee. My objective hands me a third cup, still steaming.

- You see?" he laughs. We knew you'd come!

I rip out my earpiece and sigh:

- You fooled me. I was delayed by a bottle...

- The fatal weapon!" laughs Yacouba.

- In filoche, unless someone commits a crime in front of you, and even then, nothing should distract you from your goal," pontificates Zied.

- Stop it, man!" laughs Yak. She got off easy. I was hoping I'd be rid of her by Chatelet.

My turn to laugh.

- I must admit, I bit! It was vicious, maybe too much so...

Without realizing it, I'm taking part in the first *debriefing of* my life as an RG agent.

When, a few sips of coffee later, I plug my phone back in, I realize that Malik has called me. I go out and call him back. He's in a state. He's devastated by his work.

- I'm sick of playing the chaouch," he rants. Do you think this is a life for me, bringing in breakfast? I'm sick and tired of being a low-class slave. I've got to change jobs or I'm going to lose it!

- Did you send out any applications?

- I didn't get *an* answer! Not one, can you believe it? I imagine that as soon as guys see "Malik Lakheal" at the top of your CV, it's straight to the garbage can.

- Did you redo your CV? Is it clean?

- That's why I'm calling. Can you spare a couple of s'condes to take a look at the thing and freshen it up a bit since you went to college and are working?

- You want to come over?

- No, Mom suggested you come by tomorrow night. It's for Dad.

- What's wrong with him now?

- You'll have to help him fill out his pension and tax forms, I think. What time should I tell them you'll be here?

- Pfff, I don't know. I don't have fixed hours.

- Hey, just because you're working doesn't mean you have to forget the family, Nora!

I sense that Malik has just switched to "provocation" mode. Yet I fall for it, whistling in outrage:

- Do I seem to have forgotten the family?

- Well, a little, anyway. Admit it, you're not around much.

- Because I've got my life, Malik, just as you should have yours! For the record, whenever you call me, that is, whenever you need anything, I'm always there. True or false?

My brother feels he may have gone too far, and he needs my services. So he remains silent for a few fractions of a second before making what seems, by his standards, to be a *mea culpa*:

- Yeah, maybe.

- There's no "maybe", I won't forget you. Come on, I've got to go. Tell your parents I'll be there tomorrow evening, when I can, to take care of Dad's papers and your CV.

I hang up and return to the bar. Yacouba and Zied had paid the bill and were about to take off.

In the street, they tell me we've just been assigned a mission. For tomorrow. My heart leaps with joy: a mission "for real", in which I'm going to take part, means I've passed my test. From now on, it's not just a game. We're going to have to hit the ground running. Exactly the kind of challenge that transcends me!

34.

Today's mission - my first mission! - is to follow a man called Mohamed. I don't know much about him. I have his photo, his date and place of birth, his place of residence, his criminal record (not very extensive) and his occupation. Mohamed is a thirty-five-year-old North African. He wears glasses and a goatee. A single man with no children, he works as a cleaner. His associates worry our hierarchy. He is surrounded by confirmed terrorists. It's up to us to build his environment.

Yak explains that this approach is doubly characteristic of our work at Information.

On the one hand, we are almost never aware of the ins and outs of our assignments. We are only involved at a few key moments in the cases we are entrusted with. We don't get the full picture, either before, during or after the assignment. It's a way of protecting ourselves and concentrating on our task. What happens after our investigations, we generally learn from the newspapers, when a network is dismantled!

On the other hand, our primary task is to discover and even map the frequentations of targets that enter our radars. That's what we call "creating an environment". Terrorist networks often operate horizontally. In other words, even if an individual may appear insignificant or harmless, he or she may be connected to a friend of a friend of a friend who, in turn, knows the person capable of perpetrating a terrorist act. By working on a Mr Nobody's relationships, we can spot dangerous individuals and understand who their supporters are, what their issues are and what dark designs they have.

The *brief* submitted to us is as silly as can be. Mohamed has an appointment at Porte de la Chapelle with a young Algerian fresh from the boondocks. We know nothing about this person. The aim is to take a photo to identify him. Period.

Our group is pulling out all the stops. Zied is in the soum, the famous "submarine" van with one-way windows. Jean-Baptiste is on his motorcycle. Commandant Thierry is supporting us with Sacha, a colleague who has come to reinforce the system. Yacouba and I are in charge of the pedestrian rope. Opposite the metro station, I spot my ideal vantage point: a bar. For the first time in my life, I force myself to opt for a mint diabolo, then position myself against the window. Ready to pounce, I take care to pay for my drink on the spot. Over the radio, I learn that Yacouba has positioned himself in front of the Post Office. More than an hour later, nothing has happened. In order to vary the pleasures and not irritate the boss, I order and pay for a coffee.

12 h 15. Yacouba announces the arrival of our duo... who settle into the bar where I'm sitting, just a meter away from me.

- Zied, photos! orders the commander.

Although I'm less than a metre from the targets, no matter how hard I listen, I can only hear the exclamations punctuating their conversation. Through the glass, I catch a glimpse of the stranger. He's in his twenties and wears Ray Ban glasses. His hair is short. He seems to be missing an incisor. I decide to complete Zied's work by taking a photo with my cell phone... when a guy enters the counter, puts down his briefcase and orders a coffee.

I'm appalled. It's our family doctor who's come to pour himself an *espresso* at the edge of the zinc. What's the problem? He's known me since I was thirteen. In other words, if he sees me, I'm toast. I'm too afraid that he'll exclaim, with the thundering bonhommie of a Tunisian:

- Noraaaaa! So, police, how's it going?

If the guys we're dealing with are terrorists, the mellow atmosphere of the café is likely to change completely when they discover that we're already chowing down on them! Rather than run away, I prefer to anticipate, stand up and walk towards him. With a wave of my index finger, I tell him to be quiet, then kiss him and tell him I'm on an incognito mission. Blown away, he says:

- Can I buy you a coffee anyway?

I shake my head and promise her that next time we'll have Tunisian fricassee.

- Ha, with pleasure!" he exclaims. I'm counting on it!

He whistles his little black and goes back to his consultations. I return to my seat and pretend to take a photo of myself, while in reality I'm strafing our targets with my laptop. If the mission was to discreetly take photos of the acolytes, between the soum and me, there should be enough to fill a few hard drives with our booty.

Twenty minutes later, Mohamed gets up and goes to the counter to pay. The man with the Ray Ban pulls back his chair. I whisper their imminent exit. The colleagues acknowledge receipt, then the commander announces the end of the mission.

It doesn't take long for the analysis unit to put a name to Mohamed's friend. His name is Amine, and he's a cleric known for his radical preaching. The commander seems very pleased. The proof: he doesn't react. For him, it's the equivalent of an explosion of joy.

I'm relieved and proud. When evening comes, I still have the family chores to do.

The ambivalence of my feelings returns. On the one hand, I feel it's only right to help my family; on the other, I think that, by now, everyone should be able to take care of themselves - and maybe my help is encouraging them not to become independent. Maybe it even gives them an excuse to get together! Similarly, on the one hand, I'm happy to see them again, even if it's only for a functional occasion; on the other, I sometimes wish they'd think of me just because they feel like spending a moment with me. I'm not stupid enough to believe that such a miracle will ever happen; however, my bitter lucidity isn't enough to extinguish my hope. Go figure...

35.

Fortunately, I'm passionate about my work. And it's all the rage right now.

Two days after our trip to Porte de la Chapelle, we're on duty at the Château Rouge metro station. The eavesdroppers hinted at a new rendezvous on the horizon. Yacouba and I are requisitioned for the pedestrian line. I change my appearance slightly: no more loose hair, like the other day. On the other hand, big glasses on the tip of my nose to give the impression I'm not wearing anything. When I dress up, I think of Salvador Dalí, who, when asked why he wore his incongruous moustaches, replied:

- It's to go incognito.

After having his little effect, he explained:

- Thanks to this stratagem, only my whiskers are visible. You can't see the back of me.

When I put on my big glasses, I pick up exactly on his trick: you can only see them, you can't see me behind them!

On the spot, I position myself on one side of the exit, near a hallal butcher's shop. Yak is tanned opposite, in front of a fabric store. The commander, Sacha and Jean-Baptiste are in a vehicle below.

Like good field cops, we start by being patient. Patience is not in my nature - I don't know if it's in the nature of any sane person; without much result, my job helps me work on this flaw.

On this particular day, to ease my boredom, I'm lucky. I'm in a working-class neighborhood, not far from Barbès either. I know the codes and I love the atmosphere. What's more, I don't have to worry about anyone noticing you in the big cities. It's easier to get away with it. However, an old chibani is about to shatter my illusions of discretion. He spots me, smiles at me... and pulls out his key with an impish air that makes me want to vomit. This fat pig has mistaken me for a prostitute and invites me into his bachelor pad. I give him the family middle finger. Instantly, the joker disappears, sheepish.

As for me, I'm past the anger and realize that I haven't finished deconstructing my clichés. This morning, I'm facing two for the price of one. On the one hand, I'm fighting against one of my co-religionists, who probably wants to carry out an attack in the name of a faith we share and which should therefore bring us closer together. On the other hand, I'm discovering that among the chibanis, there are also perverts. I used to make this category of human beings sacred, thanks to my father...

Suddenly, Yacouba announces the arrival of our target. Indeed, the next moment, I recognize Mohamed's silhouette. The man wears a light blue djellaba over gray jogging bottoms. What's more, he's sporting the little detail without which a Salafist wouldn't be a Salafist: visible white socks with Nike shoes of the same color. As he exits the staircase, he seems to be waiting for his colleague. Amine is not long in coming. The two men greet each other and set off at a brisk pace towards Barbès.

I'm on the front line. Yak stays further back. I'm lucky enough to master the topography. I soon understand where they're going.

- From Nora, we take Rue du Soleil.

- Copy that, Nora.

- They head for the mosque. Yak, is it time for prayer?

- No, the next one's in two hours.

- OK. They are about to enter the place of worship. I get in behind them.

I open my little handbag. I pull out my emergency hijab. I don't know what I'll be able to glean, since men and women are separated in the prayer room. Nevertheless, with a bit of luck, the guys will have stopped in what is still a mixed area, serving as a *hall* or central courtyard.

Before entering the mosque, the two men glance left and right, proving that they're not sitting still. For me, it's an encouragement: we're in the right place at the right time. What peaceful-minded believer would check if he wasn't being followed before going to pray to his Creator?

I put on my hijab. A devotee greets me, without any particular suspicion. My simplified hijab does the trick! I spot my targets. They follow a guy (an "xh", as we refer to unknown men) who opens up for them in a small room. Quickly! Find an excuse to wait for them to come out! Running out of ideas, I come up with the first: I spend a long time looking for something to put in the *zakat* box, which is intended to be redistributed to the poor. All I find is five euros. As a Muslim, I think I'm a bit stingy, but I'm short of cash. Problem is, my targets still don't come out.

I have to resort to the Hungarian proverb which suggests that, "if your sword is too short, lengthen it by one step". To my first stratagem, I add a second strategy, both opportunistic and sincere: I recite the *shahada*. And I'm convinced that Allah is grateful, because just as I finish my prayer, I see our targets emerge with a sports bag. I inform my colleagues that, this time, Yacouba will have to take over the tailing while I remove my veil and glasses.

After my transformation, Nora-the-chameleon is back on the road. The team heads for the Barbès-Rochechouart metro station. In this difficult terrain, Yak and I are sent to the front line. Jean-Baptiste and Sacha act as a safety net.

On the platform, everything is fine. The two targets are chatting. They don't seem worried or under pressure. The situation becomes complicated when a drug addict comes to Yacouba for help. Yacouba has trouble getting rid of the louse. When the train arrives at the platform, I manage to slip casually into the target car. Phew, Yacouba's boarded too. I tip my invisible hat to Jean-Baptiste and Sacha, whom I haven't seen. No doubt they're in the back car.

Trying to be as discreet as possible, I scan the targets intermittently. I know I have to be as inconspicuous as possible. The first time I feel myself being targeted, I disappear. My three colleagues will follow. At the other end of the car, I see Yacouba, and a thought crosses my mind: "It's incredible, isn't it, that here we are, he, the grandson of a Senegalese tirailleur, and I, the granddaughter of a Tunisian tirailleur, following in the footsteps of our ancestors and, in our own way, taking foolish risks to protect and serve France?"

You have to wait until Montparnasse station, over half an hour, for people to get moving. Believe me, more than half an hour of hypervigilance while pretending to nod in boredom is exhausting and takes a very, very long time. The lenses come out of the train. Filched by Yacouba (I stay behind), they thread their way through the long corridors. Direction one of the exits, then a sandwich shop. Yak enters too. He sees the guys setting up at the back of the place with the guy who must be the boss. From their bags, they pull out books and a folder crammed with documents. An hour later, Yak gives us the go-ahead: the targets come out. They greet each other. They separate. This wasn't supposed to happen!

Yak chooses his side. He asks Jean-Baptiste and Sacha to tail Mohamed, who is heading for the metro, while he follows Amine, who is heading for the station. I immediately announce over the airwaves that I'm seconding Yacouba. My intuition tells me that this is *the* lead we must not drop. It's likely that Mohamed will return home to Château Rouge. Commandant Thierry is furious. For him, Mohamed was the target. Too bad, with my colleague, I assume. I trust my instinct as a hunter, developed by several years on the force, and that of Yacouba, whose attitude and efficiency I like. We'll do the sums this evening.

Yacouba doesn't let Amine out of his sight or out of his shoes... except to glance at the destination board. Too many. Impossible to guess the right one. Amine buys his ticket at the counter - in those days, it was done! - and leaves. I immediately cut the queue and presented my police card.

- Madam, for which destination did you just sell a ticket?

- Valenton-sur-Seine.

(No, the city doesn't exist, and neither does Rue du Soleil in Barbès. Readers will understand that, while all the anecdotes in this book are strictly true, some toponyms and names have been changed).

I thank the attendant and call Yacouba back. On our cell phones, ten attempts to call the commander. Only one SMS: "RDV Beauvau. Hurry!"

We're heading back to base. We don't feel we've lost any ground. However, we're expecting a blowback. Didn't we contravene the plan to focus on Mohamed? We're not disappointed by the welcome we've received.

- Yakouba, Nora, any explanations?" spits the commander as soon as the debriefing begins. I've been running around Paris like an idiot for *nothing*; you haven't accounted for *anything*; you've abandoned the priority objective for *nothing...*

- Well, no, Commandant, not for nothing," objects my sidekick. We know that Amine left with books and documents.

- Yacouba, are you kidding me? What do I care?

I intervene - not very proudly, but I intervene:

- Amine left for Valenton-sur-Seine with books and documents.

Our boss stops just as he's about to continue his vituperations. He looks electrocuted.

- You said he was going to...

- In Valenton-sur-Seine.

- Don't move. I'm not finished with you yet. I'll be back in a minute.

Without understanding, we see him rush into the commissioner's office. About five minutes later, he emerges with his usual look of good and bad days.

- Nora, do you know where Valenton-sur-Seine is?

- Uh... no.

- And you, Yacouba?

- No, I don't.

- No matter. You'll have time to find out. Go and pack. We're leaving tomorrow to live there for a while.

36.

6:30 the next morning. I finish getting ready. It's a beautiful day. I love these early mornings in Paris. Getting up early stings, but what a joy it is to be in the city you love, in front of a blue sky where the luminosity increases by the minute and seems to illuminate you from within! I feel good about myself. I'm thrilled to be leaving on my first long-haul mission. I'm as happy as if I were going on vacation, except that I'm going to work... and I'm not necessarily going to spend my vacations in Valenton-sur-Seine.

Last night, I gave Malik the spare keys to my apartment. Officially, I wanted him to "take a look" at my apartment and look after Pipuce, my cat - an adorable grey companion with green eyes, who can't get enough cuddles. What I really want is for him to have a place of his own and escape the castrating atmosphere of the family apartment. It's up to him not to smoke under my roof. No drugs in my home, that's our contract, and that's the other unavowed aim of the operation: if his stay in my apartment can help him become an adult, who's going to complain?

I put on a little white top, black pants and a linen jacket to conceal my gun. It's autumn, but the weather feels like an Indian summer. With my sneakers on, I pack my suitcase and select a book. Opting for a safe bet, I grab Immanuel Kant's *Fundament of the Metaphysics of Morals*. I add the paperback version of the

Koran: it's about time I got to grips with it! And, at the last minute, I'm taking Friedrich Nietzsche's *Ainsi parlait Zarathoustra* with me... especially as the end of the book seems to resonate with what I'm going through right now.

> - This is my dawn. My day begins. Arise, arise,
> O high noon!
> So spoke Zarathustra; and he left his cave, fiery
> and strong as the morning sun rising from the dark
> mountains.

Like Zarathustra at his rebirth, a breath of mingled excitement and euphoria rises in my chest... but my phone brings me back down to earth, vibrating. It's Yacouba.

- Madame's carriage has arrived," he announces.

I hurry to join him in the street, and take advantage of the journey to ask him how a mission like this is going.

- There's only one rule: get meticulously organized so that we're always ready to take off from our base. At least this time, thanks to you, we'll have less trouble sticking to the target...

- That's nice, but why?

- We needed an Arab to help us out. When you're frogmarched around mosques, it's better to have someone who blends in, who knows the language, the culture, the codes, who seems to be from the seraglio, you know... Plus, a woman is clever: the target will be even less suspicious. A woman is harmless!

- So, for once, it's valued to be a chick and an Arab? It doesn't happen that often... Do you have that kind of feeling, too, as a black man?

- Honestly? No. You're popular because, apart from the essential fact that you work well, you're a chick.

- And?

- Well, even if they cut you from time to time to prove to themselves that they've got it, big macho guys tend to want to protect you. Especially as you're pretty, and let's face it, that doesn't spoil anything. I'm a guy, but I don't really like the atmosphere in rugby dressing rooms; I'm black and, what's worse, I'm a practicing Muslim. Basically, I'm a designated volunteer whenever someone's needed for something that's fun for everyone, and I'm adored when I prepare mafé.

- Doesn't it piss you off?

- Well, when it pisses me off, I say so. But my status isn't fixed, you know. It changes according to circumstances.

- What do you mean?

- Case in point? When I pray at the mosque, for the mission, I'm a golden guy. They'd almost cook mafé for me - almost! On the other hand, when I pray in the guesthouse, where we live on top of each other, I'm a retard, a superstitious or a colleague who could tip over into fundamentalism at any moment.

- It's crazy! Deep down, how do you feel about it?

Yacouba bursts out laughing.

- I work for the Republic," he explains, "and because the job I'm given seems right and I'm passionate about it. I learned a long time ago that I shouldn't expect any recognition, either from my bosses or my peers. I never do. They can give you a little bravo here and there, just like they give pigeons a piece of bread. You see, if I have any advice to give you, even if it's a bit pretentious to "give advice" to someone who hasn't asked for anything: work for yourself. For the pleasure of completing missions. For your own personal fulfillment. And for the ideal that drives you. Don't work for others. You'd be disappointed I nod. In the second section of the *Foundations of the Metaphysics of Morals,* the philosopher praises "the autonomy of the will as the supreme principle of morality". According to him, "the principle of autonomy is the sole principle of morality" and even what he called "a categorical imperative". I like the idea that our actions should be based on a universal perspective, i.e. that we shouldn't act only *for* or *by* ourselves (in order to achieve immediate happiness, for example), but in a perspective that goes beyond us - in this case, the republican principle that subsumes my work as a policewoman.

I really live it that way. I'm happy if my work is appreciated by my colleagues and superiors. However, what drives me is nothing other than the desire to be useful and to act for the common good. I can't wait to put these principles into practice in my new theater of operations!

37.

After a two-and-a-half-hour drive, I can't wait to get back to our fine team and get back to work.

We've arrived at a grayish farmhouse planted in the middle of some greenery. A white gate opens automatically on our arrival. I can see that the gîte has been carefully chosen: four cars can be discreetly parked here. At this stage of the mission, the atmosphere is relaxed. Under an arbour, colleagues are sipping lemonade. Add a few cicadas, a bottle of rosé and a smoky barbecue, and you'd think you were on vacation in the South of France.

- Incredible!" exclaims Jean-Baptiste. Yacouba has managed not to get lost for once! Nora, you've changed it for us...

- Come on," says Zied, opening the trunk of the car to grab my suitcase. I'll show you to your room. You're lucky: you're the only one with your own room *and* shower. The commandant has spoiled you.

I discover my new home, about fifteen square metres. Monastic atmosphere: white walls, wardrobe, bed in the middle with bedside table, window, shower-toilet area, period. I thank Zied, then, in order not to let myself be overwhelmed by the little blow to my morale I've just suffered at seeing where I'm going to spend the next few weeks, I set about putting my things away. On one side, my street clothes; on the other, my work gear

- djellaba, hijabs, Koran, prayer mat, radio, earpiece, handcuffs. The essentials, nothing more. I carry only my gun, my ID card and my armband.

I join the boys to quench my thirst in turn, and then we set off like tourists to do some initial scouting around Valenton. We call it "making a physiognomy".

The town is just a quarter of an hour from our base. Its medieval remains and delightful churches add to its charm. There's nothing to suggest that a major terrorist plot is afoot! As we wander around, I notice that people seem calmer than in Paris... and more mixed. I'm sensitive to this detail because, where I live, people of the same origin often congregate or are congregated together.

Openness to others" and "living together" are hollow formulas, rarely effective. I'm perplexed when I hear decision-makers crowing about them. In fact, the urban policies of the last forty years have been largely responsible for the ghettoization of our areas, and the so-called "social mix" projects perpetuate these errors. By housing only poor families who look alike in low-rent buildings, we curb the desires, possibilities and opportunities for sharing, discovery and genuine cross-fertilization between people. It prevents any desire to form a society with someone who doesn't look like me. Finally, it's about developing community reflexes that make withdrawal into oneself seem natural, logical and necessary, when in fact it's only the result of inappropriate choices guilty of contributing to the fragmentation of our society.

Our first approach to the city over, we head back to the B&B. I'm delighted to learn that I'll be seeing our target with my own eyes this afternoon. At 6 p.m., I have an appointment with Nasser...

but he mustn't know! Before the fateful hour, I record as much information as I can about him. I read his locker. I see that he has just been released from prison, which is always worrying for this type of defendant, because a terrorist who has committed attacks cannot be de-radicalized. Indeed, there is no *risk of* deradicalization, since the word "deradicalization" does not cover any reality. Even today, it barely benefits psychologists in need of recognition who, since 2015, have been squabbling to define *the* Perfect Evaluation Grid to distinguish radicalization and deradicalization in a binary way. I wish them luck!

On leaving the mosque, Nasser is on time. For the first time, I see "my man". The one to whom my existence is momentarily devoted. And to say the least, I find him marked. Prison? By his anger? By his spirit of vengeance? God knows. One thing's for sure: he's thirty-five but looks at least twenty years older. He's even more bent than he is stooped. It's as if he's carrying the weight of the world on his shoulders.

Surprised at first that a successful preacher would shine so little in appearance, I guessed that, through this posture of wise old man indifferent to his little reputation, he could more easily attract young people in search of a father or landmarks. And if you want to be seen, Nasser is seen! He sports an impeccably Salafist look: very short hair, long beard, black *jogging* bottoms pulled up to the calf to reveal white socks and typical sneakers. It's a code we mentioned earlier, and here's how to decipher it.

Salafists idealize the time of the prophets, roughly speaking: the 6th century. In those days, the rich wore long coats that reached to the ground. According to the rigorists, "the ancients" were careful to roll up their clothes to distinguish themselves from the ostentation of people who placed pecuniary wealth above spiritual wealth. The modernization of the phenomenon, the rolled-up *jogging suit,* makes laughable what once made sense. I call the result "the Tintin *look".* For me, it's a sign of the imposture of the fundamentalists.

How can we justify the impossible? These people who claim to be returning "to the origins", to the point of preferring to scrub their snags with siwak rather than a toothbrush, have cell phones - often iPhones - that I'm afraid the Prophet didn't have. These people who denounce Western society ostensibly wear Nike, a comma that symbolizes it to the utmost. That's why these faquins horrify me. If someone's interpretation of Islam differs from mine, that's fine... as long as they're consistent. They aren't. I have yet to determine whether Nasser's life is consistent with his rigorist appearance. Poor guy, he can count on me to find out!

No time to lose. I follow him as soon as he leaves the mosque. He seems to be mumbling into his beard - given the hairy extension of the individual, I've never heard the expression so apt. Concentrating on my work, I stick to the man's train, without forgetting to give him a fifteen-metre margin. I know that, further on, a subject is ready to move towards his home to photograph him entering his building. As soon as I'm sure, I indicate the direction we're taking.

- From Nora to all, Nasser has just entered the "O'dwich" kebab shop. He greets three Salaf-type individuals.

I stop nearby. Shortly afterwards, I see Zied behind the wheel of the soum, struggling to park - a classic soum driver. Over the airwaves, Jean-Baptiste, sitting in the tank, informs me that he's about to photograph the quartet after all.

I look around. There's no bench nearby. But I can't stay in the street forever. The risk of being spotted is too great. I see a leather goods shop nearby. I announce that I'm going to leave and wait for Zied's top before resuming my hunt.

In the boutique, the Asian saleswoman gives me a funny look as soon as I enter, as if she thinks I'm a thief. I point to a handbag model and sing its praises. It's beautiful and looks very practical, but I'm looking for an accessory where I can put all my stuff. I ask her if she has a slightly larger model. Stiff as a board, arms folded, without batting an eyelid, the shopkeeper tells me no. I open the bag and pretend to examine the seams with approval.

- And something similar but a little more...

- We haven't," snaps the lady.

I nod, grumbling as if I were gambling my life on this decision:

- Ah, it's a shame, isn't it... I hesitate, I hesitate...

Fortunately, Zied frees me when he announces:

- The lens comes out.

- I'll take it," I said.

On hearing this, the saleswoman smiles... then is dismayed when I put the bag down and leave the store without saying hello. As far as I'm concerned, she no longer exists. I'm a dozen meters behind Nasser and, from now on, he's the only one who counts. The man looks peaceful and walks slowly towards his council flat. He lives in a six-storey building on the outskirts of town. I let him into the stairwell. I wait a few minutes, then slip in after him. I spot his name on the mailboxes.

- From Nora to all: individual housed at 23, rue Marie Curie. According to BAL, apartment 302.

- You even have the apartment? Good work, Nora! Raise the dispo.

I get out and walk away as if nothing had happened. Yet a new *rush of* pride comes over me. I haven't been fooled; I've been able to improvise; I haven't lost my aim; I've had the presence of mind to check his apartment number. So many good points for me!

However, I don't know that this shadowing is only the first episode of a surveillance that will last eighteen months...

38.

Week after week, we spend our time in the field. When we're not out in the field, we're training relentlessly - except for Yacouba, who alternates between pillow failure, poor form and the desire to preserve himself "so as to be at the top of his game when it counts". It's to his advantage that he, who doesn't really appreciate physical effort, finds himself protected by his lazy persona, which doesn't really correspond to reality; and he's no worse off for it.

As for me, I've always had a sporting temperament. Since the Laumière club, I've never stopped boxing, even if my job hasn't always allowed me to be very regular. I took advantage of the police academy to go to the gym several times a week and, thanks to the quality of the coaching, I've seen clear progress. At the Préfecture and the twentieth arrondissement police station, my staggered working hours weren't compatible with the class timetable, so I made do by signing up for all the sports courses I could get my hands on. In Valenton, we run ten kilometers every morning, and then go on to strengthen our muscles, repeat technical movements and take on opponents. One morning, shortly after our forty-minute *jog,* Jean-Baptiste calls out to me:

- Say, Nora, I hear you're the ring slayer. Would you like to put on the gloves?

- You bet! Except that I didn't bring my own...

- Taratata, don't worry, we'll lend you some. But we don't have any mouth-guards. You'll have to be careful I don't destroy your pretty smile.

- It works!

Jean-Baptiste trots off to get some gloves. When he returns, his eyes are sparkling. I can tell he's eager to try out the new one. The challenge is well attended: Zied has pulled up a chair to comfortably watch the show, and Yacouba - who unfortunately missed the day's *running* - has joined him. The spectators are attentive and warm. The first cheers fly, accompanied by the expected mockery.

- Don't damage her too much, JB," exclaims Zied. We need her later.

- Nora, please don't humiliate him," begs Yacouba. If you do, he'll be in a bad mood again, and that's a real pain...

Facing a colossus doesn't impress me. On the contrary, I enjoy it. I'm not worried about fighting, and I'm confident in both my technique and my fitness.

As soon as I'm greeted, I'm on the alert. The assault begins. After a few insignificant skirmishes, Jean-Baptiste unleashes his first big blows to take the preferred position and dash my hopes. Strong players often adopt this strategy when they come up against lower-ranked opponents: first, they announce what they're up against, then they let it come, thinking that they've shown their power, which should dampen their opponent's ardor. I don't accept this *deal*. Jean-Baptiste's ease of movement, strength and fluidity remind me of Aymeric, but this time I'm not going to let myself be outflanked.

For this, the first thirty seconds are decisive. Thanks to the maturity I've acquired since that fatal assault, I'm very attentive from the outset, enabling me to parry heavy hooks and virile right hands. Jean-Baptiste doesn't feign: he delivers the blows. I appreciate this mark of respect. He doesn't take me for a weakling. He treats me like a colleague. Considering the beast, I was expecting a less *fair* fight.

I take his first big potatoes and, having learned to box by stepping back, I fight back in my stride. I don't want to reap without sowing. My pugnacity triggers Yak's howls:

- Go, Nono! You're the best!

- Hey, there's a match on! shouted Zied.

Out of the corner of my eye, I see other colleagues coming out of their rooms, attracted by the noise. I decide not to give my adversary a moment's thought and set off at once. As a lightweight, I have no choice but to play on speed and mobility. That doesn't mean I can't be toned. My *vista* helps me to do this: two piston-like right hands go straight through and land on my opponent's face. With a fearsome reflex jab, he pushes me away, but I'm euphoric to feel him offended.

Buoyed by a good dynamic and the encouragement that sustains it, I play David against Goliath and harass him to prevent him from developing his *punch*. Making sure I'm always on the move, I refuse direct confrontation. I wouldn't stand a chance in a pitched battle, but boxing isn't a street fight, it's a noble art. Contrary to the muscular appearances of the most famous heavyweights, finesse, strategy and technical skill all play their part.

As I circle my opponent, parrying his fearsome hooks, looking for openings, I repeat to myself: "Think of Mohamed Ali, Nora. No fatigue. No pain. Fly like a butterfly, sting like a bee. Come on, punch!"

My years of training are paying off. When the two minutes are up, the applause starts. In the hug Jean-Baptiste gives me, I feel I've earned his respect. He offers to box with me twice a week during our stay, confirming that he has enjoyed our exchange. I accept enthusiastically, then realize that the commander has seen our demonstration. I have the fleeting impression of having surprised him... even though he simply reminds me that a mission is underway, so this is no time to be on sick leave. I bow my head and reply:

- Yes, sir.

There's a time for polemics, and a time for respecting the hierarchy!

39.

Training us is one of our obligations. But the most important thing, of course, is to work with Nasser.

As the months go by, I manage to get a better grasp of the character's logic and workings, beyond his *pedigree*. Impressive *pedigree*: our target is a terrorist figure. In the 1990s, Nasser fomented attacks to "punish France for its interference in Muslim countries". Serious stuff! Born in France, our target studied and graduated. Then he got involved in the voluntary sector but, feeling discriminated against, he felt that, no matter what he tried, he'd always be a victim of "délit de sale gueule". Instead of fighting to change things, he found his reason for living in a deep-seated hatred of his homeland. To feed it, to feed *himself,* he embraced the radical ideology of jihadist Salafism.

It grows out of frustration. To those who feel rejected by society, to those who feel they have no prospects, it offers a narrative of self-worth. It offers to transform a victim into an actor. At the end of the day, it gives transcendental endorsement to violence, destruction and mass murder. It moralizes ignominy. It hallalizes mass murder.

Once this is understood, psychology has no place in our work. The choices made by Islamist terrorists are not the result of mental deviance. They draw their virulence from objectifiable realities. Deciphering their environment and describing the failures or flaws in their socialization are the best tools available. For example, when we see that many young people have left for Syria from Trappes or Lunel, sociology is likely to shed light on the process that has enabled or even encouraged, locally, the development of these epidemics of voluntary exile... in the hope of acting to prevent history repeating itself. Indeed, "acts of violence" often reveal identifiable sociological patterns. Whether Nasser, Khaled Kelkal or the Kouachi brothers, they all repeat the same story, based on similar frustrations and the dangerous illusion that terrorism will enable them to regain control of their lives.

A poor illusion, really. Like the one I'd created for myself to imagine the life of a terrorist. I was expecting a hectic *schedule*. In the morning, intensive training in the woods, survivalist style. In the afternoon, shooting practice. In the evening, Koranic classes with chemistry option for those who want to handle an explosives belt with the requisite gentleness. The reality is much less hectic.

Nasser gets up at 5:30 a.m. to go to the mosque. He returns home where, from what we can discover, he seems to have three main occupations:

- to read,

- take a nap and

- listen to France Culture.

Yes.

He returns to the mosque for the evening prayer, and then goes home.

In other words, for ten months or so, we were bored out of our minds. As we could be called up at any time, alcohol was forbidden; and when we did get leave, we were so exhausted by the crazy schedules and the hypersolictation of our concentration that we programmed ourselves two activities to the exclusion of all others: rest and laundry. We are absorbed by our mission. As Søren Kierkegaard points out, "someone who despairs despairs *of* something"[12]. But we have to admit that we're the opposite. We don't despair of anything, but we do hope *for* something.

Even though I love parties, I don't have the energy for it. As a result, I'm becoming monomaniacal. And it's not without consequences: my circle of friends and acquaintances is getting thinner. Many close and very close friends are drifting apart. At first, I don't even realize it. I'm totally focused on my mission, including the days *off* when I have only one obsession: recovering so I can be operational as soon as I get back to Valenton.

No, that's not true. I'm oversimplifying. Once, after we'd been through a week of high tension, the four of us got back into a car and, on the ring road, I pointed to the first exit to a Paris gate and said:

- Yak, we're going out there.

My colleague complied. I pointed to an open spot and decided:

- You park here.

- But... why? Don't you live in the eighteenth?

- There's a bistro across the street. I can't take it anymore, let's have a drink.

It was nine o'clock. I have to admit: when we left the bar at midnight, there was more than blood in our veins.

To occupy the rest of the time, between

---

12. Søren Kierkegaard, *La Maladie mortelle, in: Œuvres*, t. II, trans. Régis Boyer and Michel Forget, Gallimard, "La Pléïade", 2018, p. 763.

- a boxing session,

- a Koranic or philosophical reading, and

- a spinning mill,

I'm lucky enough to have found a friend in Yacouba.

During our stay, we became a stronger team. We have an obvious affinity. Yak likes to have a laugh, so do I; he likes to eat, so do I; he feels he has a personal mission to fight against the misuse of Islam, so do I; he's passionate about Islam, I'm increasingly interested. In short, one thing leading to another, we even call each other at *weekends*; we go to each other's houses for dinner; we become great friends. In fact, it seems that this job makes it easier to create duos.

Zied is very chummy with Laurent. They share the James Bond side of their *job...* and their attention to *looks*! The commander forms a double team with his officer. They manage the team and the confidentiality of the information they receive, which they have to negotiate to disclose to us. Jérôme is buddies with Jean-Baptiste. They're essentially bikers, outstanding pilots and men of action who want to help catch terrorists - but don't give a damn about Muslim culture and religion.

It may take me a while to realize it, but our differences will prove complementary. It's thanks to the specificities of each of us that we're going to try to prevent the territory from once again being the target of a bloody attack. Together, as a team, we're going to do everything we can to prevent Nasser and his henchmen from achieving their goals, and we're going to do it every day on the ground... for eighteen months!

40.

Today, as I have done almost every day for many months, I follow Nasser to the mosque. Depending on the moment, I vary my outfits. Sometimes I'm in a djellaba, other times in a blouse, *jeans* and sneakers. With or without glasses. Hair loose or tied up. Details count.

Usually, when I arrive at the mosque, I follow the target group in order to observe, as far as possible, their company, behavior and actions. To blend in, I start by saying my prayers. After that, I can wander around the building. Sometimes I find it ironic that it was the National Police who introduced me to the practice of religion!

Tonight, I attend the last *salat*, the *isha*, which is said after the last light of day has faded. Nasser is there. He greets the regulars. The man is smiling and affable. I'm sure none of those around him know his record. How and why should we suspect him of being a major killer? His appearance and assiduity assure the faithful of his seriousness; his demeanor, gentle and pleasant, makes him appreciated by all. His magnetism no doubt reinforces his dangerousness: he can seduce both by his rigorism and by the charisma he radiates. Impatient by nature, I can't wait for our work to be judged sufficiently advanced by our hierarchy for the competent services to decide to question this worrying character.

Veiled in navy blue, I enter the small place of worship. Alongside the other women, I perform my ablutions. Suddenly, I stiffen. I've just seen three individuals walk straight up to Nasser and greet him effusively. I don't know these people. But that's precisely why we stay so long under observation when a suspect is pointed out to us. By defining the target's usual environment, we are able to detect minute or discreet changes. These indicators can only be detected over a long period of time; and, often, they are highly significant when there's something fishy going on.

In other words, when the prayer begins, my mind is no longer on the four *rakats* that punctuate the *isha*. I can't wait for our invocations to end so I can get a closer look at these newcomers. I don't feel relieved until I hear the concluding formula:

- *La ilaha illa Lah, Mohamed rassoulah!*[13]

Alas, just as I'm about to bolt out of the prayer room, a woman grabs my arm. I try to pull away gently, but she insists and addresses me in Arabic.

- Are you new, Sister?" she asks.

- Yes, in a way. I've been here a few times. I like to pray here. It makes me feel good.

- *El hamdoulillah*! Welcome. My name is Latifa. You'll find a second family here. If you need anything, don't hesitate. We're here for you. Here, wait...

In spite of her kindness, I cringe inwardly as she beckons two converts to approach.

- Keltoum, Assia, may I introduce...

- Alya.

---

13. There is no God but Allah. Mohamed is his prophet.

- If you feel like it, Alya, let's meet next Thursday evening for *dars*.

The *dars*, otherwise known as "homework", are proposed by the women of the mosque. These are mini-exegeses prepared over a good meal shared with friends. Nothing formal, nothing set in stone. Like the men, the women reflect together on their daily religious practice. For example, can you pray if you're wearing perfume, or do you have to redo your ablutions?

From the big issues to the small details, everything can be approached with humility and kindness. That's why I enjoy attending these sessions, usually guided by the one who is considered the most erudite of the small group. By introducing more Western themes such as

- *coaching* for successful couples",
- children's education,
- the art of dressing, and even
- the ultra-ambitious "how to make a success of your life" debate,

dars' leaders are not afraid to innovate, helping to adapt faith to our societies and the questions they raise.

Except that, for the time being, as you can imagine, I've got other pots and pans on the stove. I thank Latifa, say hello to Keltoum and Assia, then - finally! - into the courtyard.

Phew, Nasser is still there, about to leave with his friends. I immediately tell the team:

- To all of Nora, Nasser doesn't head for home. He's turning left. I repeat, he's turning left, and he's accompanied by three people I've never seen before.

- Received, announces the commander. Yacouba, bring the soum closer. Nora, are you continuing?

- Yes, for now. Zied, be ready to take over from me just in case.

- From Zied to Nora, it's received.

- Nora, can you give me a more precise description of the surprise guests?

- One Caucasian, about six feet tall, short hair, salaf-like appearance, *sportswear*. One West Indian, about the same height. He is wearing a gray djellaba. The third, a little shorter, is NA in white Tacchini *jogging suits.* Look out, they're setting up at the *O'dwich* kebab shop. I continue on my way. Zied, do you want one?

- I got it.

- Yacouba, are you in place? asks the commander.

- I'm having trouble parking.

- It can't be! What the hell are you doing? You're not supposed to park the Pinder circus trailer! I'm warning you, I absolutely need the photo of the guys.

- I'll take care of it," says Yak in a tense voice.

A minute of silent stress. Then :

- From Yacouba to all, photo taken.

- From Zied on down, the guys are out of the kebab shop. We're approaching the mosque. Wait... They split up. Nasser heads for his apartment.

- OK, let's lift the dispo," decides the commander. Yacouba, you pick up Nora and Zied. Back to the lodge for debriefing.

As soon as we arrive at our base, we send Yak's photos to the Valenton police station. It didn't take long for the verdict to come in. Two are known for violence and drug trafficking. The other has no record. All three live in the Joconde housing estate next to the mosque.

The evening was a success. However, we're all looking forward to tomorrow. Now that we have new targets, with names and locations, we're going to get to work on them. A shiver of excitement runs through us. Will it be the intuition that our investigation has reached a decisive turning point?

41.

All hell broke loose: the in-depth investigations launched on the new suspects led to their identification... and made us realize that we'd raised the big game.

Stéphane and Marvin were born in the 1980s. They grew up in the La Joconde housing estate, where our colleagues put them up. Stéphane comes from a non-practicing Catholic family. He is an only child and never knew his father. His mother, a notorious alcoholic, left him to fend for himself from an early age. His first criminal record was at the age of sixteen.

Marvin is more precocious. Born into a West Indian family of four children and raised in the evangelical faith, this shy, good-natured boy was arrested for caravan theft at the age of fifteen. Compared to Stéphane, he's a year ahead of his time!

The third individual is called Abdelkrim. He was born in France into a family of three children. His parents are vaguely practicing Muslims - more vaguely than practicing. Father a factory worker. Mother a cleaning lady. Just like me. Except that I'm a girl. So maybe I had a better chance of making it...

Indeed, most of the time, boys born into North African families in France have a ball and chain around their necks. From their very first wail, they are considered heroes. It's not a legend, it's a reality. Everything is allowed to the little male. He's entitled to everything. He's forgiven everything. So he grows up with a sense of omnipotence that adolescence inevitably cracks. Expectations become contradictory. The mother continues to over-protect her baby-for-life; the father expects the little boy to grow up to be a good man, just as he and his companions had to become. The hard way. The less robust boys prepare for adulthood by suffering:

- on the one hand, the father's perpetual disappointment that they'll never measure up, and,

- on the other hand, nostalgia for a lost paradise where they were the gods of their family.

That's why young girls from the Maghreb generally do better than their brothers, both at school and in life. Not because, as I hear here and there, "they're smarter", but because little is expected of them. They're not at the center of the world. They live in the shadow of the men in the family. And they understand that, to get by, to live their own lives, they can only rely on their own strength of character and the opportunities for social advancement that the Republic offers, no matter what anyone says, to a certain extent.

Boys, on the other hand, often find themselves at the age of eighteen with the conviction that they're not worth much. Shunned by their fathers, infantilized by their mothers, they have to face up to a society that readily equates North Africans with scum, opening up only two specialized channels for them: *drug dealer* or Islamist.

There's nothing miserabilistic or victimizing about what I'm saying - on the contrary! The fault lies partly with us Arabs, the daughters and sons of immigrants. Out of respect for our forebears, we refuse to question the way we were brought up. We erect as a totem a mythologized past, with its reflexes sedimented in the collective memory. The result is unmistakable: we find ourselves caught between the weighty heritage of Tradition and the exclusionary gaze of the *gaouris*, as those who consider themselves native French are known in the neighborhoods.

This perpetuation is deadly. It leads many young people from the Maghreb to miss out on their potential and to conform to the caricatures we have planned for them. Believing they are rebelling against the France that despises them, they conform to deleterious stereotypes. And yet, it must be written in black and white: there is no fatality. Just the enormous weight of the past and habits.

And yet, this overwhelming Tradition is a fertile breeding ground on which a rigorist, even extremist Islam greedily germinates. This fertility has an almost simple explanation. Many young North Africans hear it said at home that the golden age of the Arabs is over. Those who go to school long enough only hear about Islam through four succinct and reductive episodes:
- the birth of the Prophet,
- expansion until the battle of Poitiers,
- the Crusades and
- colonization.

In short, the French Ministry of Education fails to mention the richness of a civilization from which many of the children in its care come. In addition to the feeling of being misunderstood, which the most virulent elements may equate with a sign of contempt or arrogance, there are key moments that feed the resentment of many Arabs, among whom four stand out:
- the massacre of october 17, 1961,
- the 1983 March of the Beurs, stolen from the community and from Toumi Djaïdja (our very own Martin Luther King!),

- the death of Malik Oussekine,

- the suppression of riots in the suburbs.

These misfortunes, these failures, these misunderstandings all contribute to fuelling the risk of mutual rejection. When Arabs are mentioned, no one refers to individual or collective successes, intellectuals or artists (apart from a few entertainment stars). That's why I'm convinced that, in the face of emptiness and desolation - some of it illusory, some of it well-founded - young people with a bad feeling about themselves have within them the seed that pushes them towards the verdant meadows of the promoters of a conquering Islam.

With these shoddy mentors, the depressed of yesteryear, bamboozled by well-honed speeches and references beyond their understanding, begin to dream of a caliphate and an empire to rebuild. The apprentice terrorists don't practice their religion primarily for themselves, to find peace, hope and communion with a community always ready to find a place for everyone. They don't believe in Allah because they're certain he's the one and only God, and it follows that giving thanks to him is a duty. They join in a project of glory and conquest; they feel part and parcel of the martial perspectives sketched out by their favorite Salafist preachers; they want to invest themselves in the Islamist reconquest that will give them, even to the point of martyrdom if necessary, the conviction of being precious, indispensable, even magnificent - which, until now, they are convinced they are *not*. At this stage of the investigation, I fear that Stéphane, Marvin and Abdelkrim, each in their own way, have followed this path.

When contacted, our BAC colleagues confirmed that they had spotted the trio. Better still, they had noticed *their absence of* late.

I salute their powers of observation. Only experienced and gifted cops are capable of seeing what they see as well as what they don't see. And there's nothing innocuous about their observation. It raises the anxiety level a notch. As soon as we record it, we call in the Border Police. Perhaps, by launching urgent investigations, they'll be able to pinpoint some of their movements?

I remember the moment Jean-Baptiste revealed the results of this express survey. I was in my room, recharging my batteries with the *funky* sounds I love. The Isley Brothers, One Way, SOS Band, it's a big part of my life! You can't imagine how much music warms the heart, even if it's looked down on by those who call themselves "the knowers".

That day, I was listening to "Outstanding", a song by The Gap Band, from their fifth album (albeit number four!). I love this distinctive song, with its bass riff and piano off-beats. Plus, as someone who feels alone in the world, a bit like SuperNora lost in the middle of nowhere to save the Republic, I'm blown away by

- the *groove of* the piece,

- the warm voice that reaches me and

- the words - silly, yes, but how I wish they were addressed to me more often!

Outsanding (So outstanding, yeah)!
Girl, you knock me out.
Excited (I'm so excited, baby),
It makes me want to shout.[14]

---

14. "You're exceptional (so exceptional). / Baby, you're stunning / You turn me on so much / I want to scream!"

JB breaks the Wilson brothers' magic by knocking on my door.

- We've got news, Nora," he announces. Two of our three love-birds have just returned from Pakistan. They spent two months there, and I don't think they had full board at Club Med. We meet in the lounge for the captain's *briefing*.

I'm stunned. I turn off the music and get ready to join my colleagues.

What's strange is that, apart from minor offences, the "loulous" Jean-Baptiste refers to were never identified as potential jihadists. They didn't attend the mosque before they left, and they didn't wear the Salaf uniform. I suspect that self-proclaimed experts will see this as a sign of *taqqya*. For me, *taqqya was* a way of concealing the practice of one's faith in order to protect oneself from persecution. This was the case in Iran, where minority Shiites had to protect themselves from the Sunnis. Unfortunately, in the 2000s, neo-specialists changed the definition of the term. Henceforth, the official understanding reduces the term to the (supposed) camouflage technique used by terrorists to conceal their criminal plans.

This theory is seductive to haters, as it allows them to see every Muslim as a potential terrorist, even if he or she lives a Western lifestyle. The nice Arab you share a drink with at the bar may be nothing less than a Khaled Kelkal trying to fool the good French. That's what the modernized notion of *taqqya is all* about. And it's as stupid as it is revolting, for at least two reasons.

First reason: all Muslim terrorists did not hide their rigorist practices before committing their crime. You don't have to eat pig to carry out a successful attack. Among Muslim terrorists, there are Muslim terrorists who look like Muslim terrorists. But that doesn't stop them from carrying out their sinister deeds. So, the "*taqqya* strategy" is just a lot of hot air.

Second reason: before their crimes, it's true that some terrorists frequented hostess bars and drank themselves into a stupor on Fridays instead of listening to sermons. However, they didn't conceal their religious practice through Machiavellianism or superior intelligence: they were simply incapable of maintaining the posture of a practicing Muslim for more than a few hours, so unnatural was it to them. In their eyes, Islam was simply a good opportunity to blow things up.

An imprecise concept, *taqqya is used as a* pretext to cast anathema on all Muslims, suggesting that behind every Muslim there is, or could be, a Muslim *brother* bent on subjugating France. *Taqqya* explains nothing. Designates nothing. And, if you stop to think about it for a moment, it doesn't undermine the credibility of Islam in France. Hardly the Islamologists on TV. Now that's justice!

42.

Since Nasser's companions have just returned from a trip to Pakistan, the red alert is on. There's not a second to lose!

We're off to the local branch of the RG. They, too, are in an uproar. They confirm that they know our new targets as young delinquents who hang around the housing estate at night. They had not detected any signs of radicalization among them prior to their departure.

A sign that times are serious, Commissaire Bernard is on deck. Good news for the officers he supervises, as this big shot has the reputation of being an uncompromising boss who stands by his decisions. Straight in his boots, the man knows how to be firm without being obtuse. He doesn't *manage* his staff: he commands those he calls his "boys" (I don't mind being one of them, on the contrary!). He doesn't care about statistics or the pretty pie charts that come into their own when you project a PowerPoint in front of the hierarchy. He prefers concrete efficiency that has a profound impact on the organizations we're tackling, rather than the kind of penny-pinching accounting we're used to. He is at the service of France, not his career. His "boys" are aware of this, and they appreciate - we appreciate - both his character and his dedication.

- Well, guys," he begins, "I'm sorry, but you won't be seeing your families, sweethearts and sweethearts any time soon. Thanks to the quality of your work, the vacations have been suspended. I'm sure I can count on you 200%. To support us, the technical group will also be fully behind us. We've already set up IS [security intercepts] on the guys we're interested in, but now we need to move up a gear. Your respective officers will tell you in detail how to proceed. Do you have any questions?"

No question, of course.

We return to the lodge, where the captain announces the battle plan. In yet another sign that we're in for an exceptional time, Thierry dares to bend the rules. To mark the occasion, he opens a bottle of Yamazaki, a highly-rated Japanese whisky, and serves a glass to each of us. The fact is as exceptional as what our glass reveals: the aroma oscillates between coconut and spice, and the taste miraculously manages to combine balance, power and persistence. Nothing to do with basic whiskies, sometimes excellent for unclogging sinuses, but whose metallic taste and violence sometimes make you wonder whether they wouldn't be better suited to starting a recalcitrant combine harvester.

I almost feel sorry for Yacouba. Because of his religious convictions, my boyfriend can't share this marvel with us. He has to stick to his personal stash of Fanta, where coconut and spice flavors are rarer. I make the best of a bad situation, thinking that, so much the better, it will leave more for the others!

- Tomorrow afternoon," announces the commander, "during the last prayer, we're going to break into Nasser's house. So we need to be sure of his position throughout the whole operation. Since we're not going to stick him with a beacon..."

He turns to me and says:

- ... you'll be the one on the hook, Nora. Alone, because there have to be three of us with the technical group, just in case. Zied, Jean-Baptiste and I will provide security for our colleagues. Yacouba will be the driver, close by.

- What if I lose it?

- I don't understand the question.

- Well... if Nasser manages to escape me, what...

- I know you won't lose it.

- If you lose it, we're dead, cousin, period," pontificates Zied.

- You won't lose it," insists the commander. There's no reason to. You've made hundreds of these. You know the guy. You know the area. And you know everything's timed. We've got twenty hot minutes, no more. The techs we get are geniuses. If you were to lose the target - and I don't believe this for a moment - you'd say so over the airwaves and we'd make our arrangements. Our lives and the success of this mission are in your hands. Do you feel up to it?

I nod, trying to look serene. What can I say to that? That I'm scared to death that, if I screw up, my colleagues might perish? Not the house style.

However, once the *briefing* was over, I ran to Yacouba to express my anxiety. He takes me by the shoulders and, looking me in the eye, says in a definitive tone:

- Don't do it. The commander *has entrusted* you with this mission. That means he *trusts* you. If he, who didn't really want a chick in the group, has confidence in you, then *you* must have confidence in yourself. Given what you've proved since you arrived, you're right to have confidence in yourself! Besides...

He stops for a moment, lets go of me and grimaces:

- If anyone has to pull a face, it's me.

- Well... why?

- I'll be in submission.

- And?

- You're going to get superhero roles, while I... Go ahead, no problem, you can call me Joe the Taxi!

I burst out laughing and kissed him, thanking him for his comradeship. His words managed to remobilize me.

The next day, I was back in warrior mode. Nora the ninja is back!

I checked my radio's battery.

I synchronized the watches with my comrades.

I have the plan in mind:

- check on Nasser's presence during the prayer,

- whether he'll stay for the *trawih*, the wake that follows,

- if he slipped away before the colleagues had finished their work and..,

- if need be, in this case, warn the guys and create an incident to delay Nasser's return, even if it means getting burned.

What happens next, you've known all along: the tricky situation, the discovery that Amine-le-redoutable is fooling around with Nasser, and Yacouba's and my fear that the commander would come down hard on us for continuing the mission a few minutes after the device was lifted.

It doesn't fail. Our boss is furious.

- Do you realize what just happened? You almost blew the whole mission to play James Bond. If the guys had destroyed you, what would you have done? I wouldn't. You were done for. Just so you know, this isn't Children's Island. We're not on Casimir's ass.

We're watching terrorists, for crying out loud, and the cream of the crop.

- But, Commander...," Yacouba tries to say.

- No "buts", just explanations. I'm curious to know what pretext you came up with to disobey my orders. Did you want to add your own personal touch? Were you frustrated? Not enough thrills for your taste, perhaps, for the day? Or is it that when I say, "Let's get this show on the road", you don't understand the meaning of certain words? Or do they? Well, that's good. Go ahead, I'm listening! I can't wait to get to the bottom of this, but beware, beware of what you're about to drool over!

I jump in to end the tirade:

- Commander, Yak had nothing to do with it.

- I don't care whether he decided or followed you. *You* disobeyed.

- *I* acknowledge that I exceeded my orders. I am the only one responsible.

- Don't care.

- Despite this, I accomplished my mission.

- Thank goodness for that!

- I never took my eyes off Nasser. At no time did I endanger anyone, not myself or a colleague.

- What if you'd been spotted?

- We weren't spotted, that's the main thing. Still, I was the leech I was supposed to be.

- So I'm angry for nothing?

- No, Commander, you're angry because I disobeyed and dragged a comrade into my fault, but listen precisely to what happened.

- I'm listening, I'm listening, I'm just listening, except that it takes you a while to spit it out, I think.

- Just as you ordered the return to base, Yacouba picked me up.

- And then?

- And then, at that precise moment, we saw Nasser get into a car with Abdelkrim. Yak recognized the driver. It was Amine. The guy we'd spotted at Porte de la Chapelle and who, at Montparnasse, took the train to Valenton-sur-Seine. We photographed the plate and picked it up.

Hearing Amine's name, our boss snapped. Inflamed ten seconds earlier, his tone reverted to its natural dryness as he scolded:

- Send me the photo immediately. This meeting is adjourned. We'll resume this conversation later.

He storms out of the living room and locks himself in his room. I hasten to send him the photo we took of the plaque. Perhaps it will earn us the grand pardon!

43.

A few hours later, confirmation came. The car's registration was in Amine's name. There's no way we're going to be able to put up with it any longer. Once again, Amine saves the day for Yak and me!

Following this discovery, some of our colleagues made our task easier. They've had him on their radar for a few weeks, and they've agreed to share their information with us. Even among fellow police officers, legend doesn't lie, and that's far from always being the case.

Amine is a bearded man. He's the father of two little girls. He works in a factory. He sometimes goes to the nearest mosque. A smooth profile, so to speak. At least in the sense that there's nothing to report since his release from prison. However, he does have one minor peculiarity: on Friday evenings, he goes out to the prostitutes waiting for customers on the outskirts of town, demands a free blow job and then extorts money from them "for the cause". In other words, after coming, he beats them up, takes their money "in the name of Allah" and keeps the girls' hard-earned cash in his pockets.

- Our colleagues are keeping Amine under their radar," says the commander. We're sticking with Nasser and his three companions. That's enough to mobilize our team. Now we have to go into overdrive. We need to beef up our case. We know that things are moving. We have to be on them all the time and never give them any slack.

I can only imagine the pressure Thierry must be under. By focusing his group for so long on Nasser, he's taken a gamble which we mustn't forget was very risky before proving to be very judicious. That notwithstanding, if, through carelessness, error or clumsiness, we let our objectives commit an attack when we've been after them for fifteen months... the backlash would be fatal!

As for me, I couldn't bear to let Amine commit an attack in the name of Islam when he's almost within our grasp. As I see it, this good apostle plays the prophet when he gets home. Rosary in hand, in the name of Allah, he has to force his family to sleep on mattresses on the floor, forbid television and dolls to his daughters... and then go off to get sucked off by peripatetic girls whom he beats up to rob after raping them. I'm disgusted by this person, because he embodies the worst deviations from my religion:

- condoning terrorist barbarism in the name of Allah, and

- the hypocrisy of the false rigorist who is only a true deviate.

Don't get me wrong, I'm a very imperfect Muslim. I don't respect all my obligations. Neither my heart nor my actions have the purity of alabaster. So I don't judge the practices of others. There's just one detail: I don't claim to be a role model and to impose a very precise code of conduct on my co-religionists that I wouldn't respect. So, without further ado, I'm glad I don't have to shadow Amine!

44.

For several weeks, focused on our objectives and dedicated to our 24/7 task, we increased the pace. Eavesdropping becomes more meticulous; the number and duration of shadowings increase. In such cases, the challenge is not to fall asleep in the routine. Experience teaches us that, as soon as we indulge in the kind of snobbish boredom that any repetitive activity can engender, disaster strikes.

But experience is (almost) always right, and it didn't take long to prove it once again.

One day, at 5:30 p.m., I'm about to follow Nasser and his three friends to the *asr* prayer. Marvin, Abdelkrim and Stéphane are dressed in fatigues as if, for them, going to pray was like going to war. Over their fatigues, they wear a gray djellaba. Each has a white fez on his head. On their feet, they wear the white Nike shoes that I don't know which ulama must have hallalized!

I follow the four men. I know that Zied is nearby and that Yacouba should be arriving with the soum.

As sometimes happens, it's best not to be in a hurry with Yak! He soon tells us he'll be a quarter of an hour late. Nothing to worry about. We know the day's fine team inside out, and it's not vital to photograph them every time.

The guys stop to chat in front of the place of worship. I land almost opposite, on a bus stop bench. It's even hotter because

I'm wearing a veil. I see the quartet enter the mosque. I decide to wait for them there. But suddenly, they turn back with a determined step.

- From Nora to all: the quartet comes to me.

- Where are you, Nora?" inquired the commander.

No time to respond. I have a split second to tear off my inductions lest my targets hear the transmissions as they get closer. It's me they're coming to.

Breathless, I hear Nasser ask me in Arabic:

- Sister, what's your name?

I lower my eyes, feigning the modesty of a very pious woman, "in the *dine*" as we say.

- Alya," I answer in a small voice. And who are you?

In response, his three acolytes start reciting religious chants in cadence. The strange melody envelops us like an eerie soundtrack. Marvin keeps looking around him and his companions. Finally, Nasser's voice resumes:

- Do you think God created you to betray your people, Alya?

I look at him in amazement. He insists:

- Aren't you ashamed to serve the enemy, as you stoop to do?

The three hummers approach me without ceasing their serenade. They stare at me in disgust. If they make a move, I won't have time to grab my gun. Damn this djellaba! I'm on my own. I'm frightened. I still want to believe that Zied and Yacouba are coming. Alas, doubt or lucidity nibbles away at my last attempts at optimism. There's no known shadow behind these four menacing figures. The situation is not looking good.

Arching, bending, stooping, Nasser leans towards me again and whispers:

- We've been on to you and your band of miscreants for months. This black man without honor and this Arab without the slightest dignity... These *keffiroune* deserve only Hell. After the Qiyamah, they will know Al Hâwiyah, where suffering is infinite. They will eat Zaqqum to burn from the inside out. But for you, it's different. Allah has chosen you. Allah has chosen you, my sister!

I fall from Charybdis into Scylla. I thought Nasser wanted to kill me; now he's trying to turn me around.

- You're a victim," he continues. A poor lost soul. It's Allah who wanted us to meet. Join us, my sister. You have the courage. Allah will give you strength. Your place is with us. Don't waste any more time. Allah has been waiting for you for so long... Can't you see how late it is?

And then, suddenly, driven by a vital impulse, without really having wanted it, without having thought about the consequences, as if in a last stand where heroism is less important than honor, I leap to my feet and say to him:

- I will never, ever follow a sick man of your hope, *takfir*!

At that moment, I think I read the hatred in his eyes. His jaw is set like a dog's ready to bite.

- You can run wherever you want, sister," he hisses. You'll never go far enough to avoid Allah's will. Repent while you can.

The bus to the Mona Lisa is coming. But has anyone escaped bloodthirsty terrorists by taking a bus? I give it my best shot. With a gesture, I get out of the way. The three acolytes get ready to intervene. With a wave of his hand, Nasser stops them. He even steps aside to let me pass.

- May Allah forgive you, sister," he says. Take care of yourself, and remember: whatever happens, you'll always be an Arab.

I go upstairs without turning around. I hear the doors close behind me. I look over my shoulder. They didn't go up. I'm alive. They spared me.

Incredulous, I feel the sweat suddenly pouring from every pore of my skin in what seems like gallons. Despite my tremors, I reach for my mobile and dial Yacouba's number.

- Pick me up at the Three Towers," I say. I'll be there in five minutes.

I hang up as quickly as possible. My only thought was to pull myself together before meeting up with my colleagues. An RG agent can't break down after being confronted by a terrorist. It wouldn't be dignified. I'll show I've got guts. I'll earn my place by my bravery and toughness. I'll prove that I'm something between steadfast and indestructible. At least, I'll try.

I'm aware that this beautiful project won't be easy to complete. When I get off the bus at the agreed stop, I'm still shivering. A few minutes later (an eternity, in other words), I see Yacouba arriving. Tears sting my eyes. I bite my tongue and promise myself I'll make it. In all circumstances, as long as I'm in front of others, I want to live up to my role.

Yacouba parks in the wild and leaps out of the vehicle. He takes me in his arms and hugs me, whispering in a faint voice:

- Thank God, Nora, you're alive! We were wondering where you'd gone. Please, don't pull a stunt like that again, promise?

I remember repeating to myself over and over again the appropriate mantra: "I'm stronger than I think. I'm stronger than I think. I'm stronger than I think." Then I remember taking a deep breath to calm myself... and bursting into tears.

45.

Back at the lodge, the team members congratulate me on my "courage"... and get ready to celebrate the end of the mission.

The end of the mission?

Still shaken by my face-to-face meeting with Nasser, I feel like I've been hit by a second wave when I hear these words. I take them back:

- What do you mean, "the end"?

- Come and have a look," says the commander, drawing me into the living room.

He shows me a huge diagram with maps, photos and arrows in every direction. I squint. I recognize every face, every place, every relationship between the protagonists. I realize that, deciphered, compiled and analyzed, our micro-observations now constitute a precise inventory of the dangers and Islamist forces gathering and plotting in Valenton.

- Our presence is no longer necessary. Nasser and his friends are surrounded. As soon as they move an ear, the colleagues will know it and beat them straight up.

I'm a little proud and a lot disappointed. Nasser is my first terrorist. Mine. I don't want to leave him to my colleagues. I know they'll do a good job, that our job isn't to arrest the accused, but I want to keep following the preacher, stay on the case and, above all, arrest him when the time comes. Don't I deserve it? Especially as it would be a nice revenge for Alya!

Suffice it to say that, during the little party that follows, I don't feel up to it. The following night, I brood. And in the morning, when we've packed our bags, set off again in silence and Yacouba has dropped me off in Barbès with my suitcases, I get a nasty case of the *blues*.

I told Malik I'd be back. He's not back. The apartment is empty. It's like seeing my life: clean, functional, incomplete, charmless. I'm back in my seventy square meters, furnished but not personalized. No one is waiting for me. No welcoming gesture. Not a flower, not a bottle in the fridge, not a word, nothing. Even Pipuce, hiding under the bed where she won't come out, pretends not to recognize me.

Just the day before, I was risking my life to track down terrorists, and now I sit uselessly on my sofa, not knowing what to do. The only things I can think of to do? Housework and shopping. The obligations of *losing*.

Just the day before, I was dutifully playing the role assigned to me by the police to help save the Republic and its innocent citizens. Today, I've been demoted to my true rank, that of a young woman who

- is not recognized by his own people,
- has no stable companion,
- lives in a soulless dwelling, and yet,
- struggles to assimilate the lesson that his malaise sends out in flashing red letters: you can't rely on work, no matter how exciting it may be.

If we risk it, the result speaks for itself, sending workaholics down the slide into the Great Depression.

All the more so as, in the short term, my professional prospects don't enchant me either. The life of an RG agent, when not on a mission, consists of working in an office. An office at Place Beauvau, yes, but an office nonetheless.

When we get caught up in it, we are dismayed. We examine current events that may affect intelligence. We deepen our knowledge of our areas of intervention. We discover the latest technical inventions. We take practical courses, for example in photography and video, or theoretical courses, for example on the evolution of Islamist currents. It's all very interesting, but more often than not, these diversions fail to contain our urgent, almost oppressive urge to leave.

At SORS, we are people of action, police officers in the field. As soon as we walk into an office and spend several hours there, we feel uncomfortable. We need the stress and adrenalin that come from being on the beat. We need to discover new places, new colleagues, new challenges and, let's face it, new spaces that liberate us from our daily routine and the people we're used to dealing with. We need to be involved in a long-term mission, where the discomforts and obligations consubstantial with the job push us to give our best... while our carefully ordered Parisian life seems insipid.

At Place Beauvau, I know what's in store for us. We're going to try to keep to conventional office hours, and if we don't succeed, we're going to burn through some of the tons of overtime we've accumulated on our missions, without feeling any freer or happier as a result. Nothing exciting.

Leaving, I decide to shake things up. I'm not going to go on undermining myself. I put on my sneakers. Direction Gare du

Nord! I don't care if it's a bit late, I'm going to be invited to lunch at my parents'.

Around the rue de Compiègne, it's swarming with dragonflies, as usual. But on this day, I'm almost glad to see them. At least they haven't moved. I'm alone, yes, but in familiar surroundings.

In my childhood apartment, my mother welcomes me Tunisian-style:

- Look, a ghost! What are you doing here? Bah, shut up, I know: you're skinny as a rail. Look at you, girl, you're a bag of bones! You're hungry, aren't you?

- OUIIIII!" I say, realizing that she's absolutely right.

- We've finished eating, but you're in luck, I think there's a bit left in the stewpot. Go and see your father while I warm up the frichti for you.

In the living room, my father sits on the sofa, his eyes riveted on yet another *Colombo* rerun. He barely deigns to turn his head slightly towards me before staring back at the television. If he missed me, he hides it masterfully.

- So, what brings you here?" he asks me in a sullen voice.

- Nothing special, Dad. I just came to pay you a little courtesy call.

He roars:

- A courtesy call? Did you think you were visiting King Hussein of Jordan? Take off your shoes and go see your brother in the bedroom.

I feel like a rugby ball that everyone is trying to pass to their neighbor: mother to father, father to son...

Nevertheless, I comply so that the televore doesn't miss a crumb of his series. On my way to the bedroom, I notice that several books on Islam have appeared in the corridor. In Malik's den, it's even worse - the shelves are full of them! So I attack them provocatively:

- Since when can you read, Malik?

- I read for my religion. Did you see that?

I look at her little library. It's full of *bestsellers made in* Saudi Arabia, like *Martine découvre le Coran (Martine discovers the Koran)*, in ten pages and large print, sold for three euros. I leaf through this rag and exclaim:

- But it sucks!

- Shut up!" says my brother indignantly. Have you no respect for Islam, you miscreant?

- On the contrary! Except that my religion has nothing to do with this nonsense, which is as dangerous as it is harmful...

- Nonsense. If it were dangerous and harmful, it would be banned, wouldn't it?

- No. We're not in a dictatorship, we have the right to express ourselves freely; and you have the right to maintain your freedom of thought. Does exercising your critical spirit mean anything to you?

- Wait a minute: if I understand what you're saying, I'm free to think that salafs are assholes, otherwise I'm a big asshole, right?

- It's *because* you're not a big jerk that I'm talking to you the way I'm talking to you, Malik. You know that rigorism is dangerous territory!

- Maybe, but before the salafs, there was nothing for us. No place to discover, enrich and strengthen our faith. Find a counter-example! Nah, don't look, there was no such thing. There was *wallouh*. Thanks to these books, I gave up *pot* and alcohol.

- That's great, but... Malik, seriously, you can't approve of people who write such *bullshit*!

- Of course not! I can't stand them. If that's what you call my freedom of thought, let me reassure you: I hate the Saudis. They're hypocrites and bad Muslims.

- So why do you buy their books?

- It's all there is. It helps me to live my religion. So you have to admit that the salafs aren't all bad after all...

- And that big Koran over there?

- Ha, that... For the past month, the Saudi Arabian embassy has been offering books to all young people. You don't have to be Salaf or even Muslim, they give you their books regardless of class or race or anything. My mates have been there. So did I. So there you go.

- Nora, taaaable!" shouts my mother from the kitchen.

- Well, we'll talk about it later," I conclude.

- I doubt it. Why don't you talk to me again when you want to get back on track?

And he concludes, with a mischievous smile that fits him like a glove:

- I've got a bit of a head start on you now, little sister. I can show you the way!

Although I know that Malik is not fooled, I'm stunned to have discovered that hate preachers and their Saudi sponsors are insinuating themselves into my family. Yet, confident in my brother's intelligence, I let myself be drawn in by the smell wafting from the ovens.

On the menu: Tunisian-style tripe with tomato and chickpeas. Another one of my favorite dishes! My spirits are lifted. Especially as the cook who prepared it for me remains, whatever his short-comings in other areas, the best cook in the interstellar world - a title that, like all Tunisian women, I definitely, without a shadow of a doubt and exclusively, award to my mother.

46.

Four weeks later, I'm feeling better. After my homecoming *blues* and a few days in the office, I decided to cut back and take some time off, like many members of our team. I know I can be called back at any time, but it doesn't matter: I'm taking the opportunity to breathe. As time goes by, I realize that I needed it. The accumulated stress and fatigue had insidiously nibbled away at my most precious possession: my joie de vivre. I conclude that I need to improve on this point. I'll have to find a balance between remaining passionate about my job (otherwise, it's impossible to do it) and preserving a space where I can exist without it (otherwise, it's impossible to last).

When I return from vacation, I'm back on my feet. I spend a day at the police shooting range, getting back into the swing of things by regaining my reflexes and sensations. The instructor is amazed that all my bullet holes are in my target's head. He advises me to be more varied: sometimes, a lethal shot isn't necessary. Personally, I don't mind putting everything in a terrorist's head, because I only want to shoot at the moment of worst danger; and in that case, it's better to be definitely effective, isn't it? I'm sure that the worst obligation for a peace officer is to be forced to use his weapon. I hope it never happens to me.

Leaving the stand, I head for the Franprix in Goutte-d'Or. I've decided to make myself a TV tray worthy of the name. As I check out, I realize that my groceries reflect my personality.

"Tell me what you buy, I'll tell you who you are!"

Now, in my basket, I put

- sandwich bread,

- a jar of hummus,

- a jar of olives,

- a hallal sausage… and

- a small châblis.

My Tunisian side, my French side.

My religious side, my irreducible side.

To tell the truth, I'm not unhappy to be the one eating hallal sausage and drinking a good glass of wine. I'm also not a little proud to be both the hard-nosed policewoman who dreams of action and danger, and the girl who sparkles inside because she's going to sit quietly at home, alone, in front of the TV with her evening snack. Of course, it's not always easy to accept yourself in all your diversity and tensions. Seeing in the *mix'n'match that* constitutes me a richness rather than a contradiction is no easy task either. However, I hope to continue learning to make my way more harmoniously.

- de Française,

- policewoman,

- woman,

- free-spirited and

- Muslim.

Arriving home, I prepare my little feast and settle down in front of the screen. I don't care what I'm watching: a good movie, a turnip, an appalling series or a reality show - tonight, anything goes! I arrive just in time for the 8 p.m. news presented by Patrick Poivre d'Arvor. Impeccable. I bite into my first hummus toast... and nearly choke on the front page.

- Today, the police carried out a major raid, announces PPDA. The aim was to dismantle a major Islamist network in Valenton-sur-Seine. At its head was a certain Nasser, a recidivist terrorist. He and his accomplices were preparing to carry out a new series of attacks on French soil.

I drop my glass of wine. As soon as I regain the use of my brain and limbs, I jump on the phone and call my favorite accomplice:

- What the hell, Yak? They hit Nasser without telling us!

- Well, so what?

- Without us, they wouldn't have had him. We could have participated in his arrest, couldn't we?

- No.

- What do you mean, "no"?

Yak sighs.

- Ha, Nora...," he murmured. Do you remember one of the first things the commander had to say to you when you landed?

- No.

- Something along the lines of: "We investigate, we get the information, we dig, *but* we don't jump the gun." Basically...

- Perhaps.

- You knew about this, didn't you?

- Anyway, I've made my decision.

- Which one?

- I'm going to ask for a transfer. I won't stay another day in this department.

- Nora…

- There is no "Nora"! I feel so frustrated tonight…

- What are you going to do? Go to the police? That'd be great. You'll type the guys up, audition them and never do the clearing-up work again. It's a shame because, in my opinion, it's the most interesting.

- But do you at least understand why I'm disgusted?

- Given your character, yes, I can imagine! Tell yourself that it's the job that's coming home to roost and that, after learning the basic techniques, after carrying out your first trials in the field, after making a brilliant contribution to the Valenton operation, you're also learning the limits of your intervention perimeter. Is it very unpleasant? So be it! Still, I've got good news for you, Nora: the shock you feel when you realize that you'll never be able to arrest the guys you're watching, means that you're becoming a full-fledged Intelligence officer. Welcome to SORS, sister!

Still in shock, I thank Yak for his friendship and heartfelt intelligence. I kiss him. Hang up. Mop up the oenological mess on my floating floor. Pour myself another glass. Try to calm down. And realize that my boyfriend and colleague is right. Even if the PJ is an idea that's been in the back of my mind since the films of my childhood (and my meeting with Aymeric made that dream come true), Yacouba is right: it's healthy for each department to have its own specialty. We can't excel in all areas at the same time. Focusing on a specific project strengthens our collective effectiveness. Coordinating our know-how guarantees the relevance of our interventions. The evening news proves it. I'm going to stay with SORS for a while longer, and then we'll see!

47.

When all is said and done, I could almost thank Nasser in turn and say something like this…

You don't know what you've brought me, "brother". So let me explain it to you in a few words.

The anger I've felt towards you and your kind has given me the strength, courage and energy to go forward and not let your hatred take over our peace, nor your destructive ideology taint my religion. Today, I'm also writing this book against you. I want, in my place and as far as I'm able, to steal your audience. I want to explain to readers of good will that you are not Islam. And I want to shake the souls you tempt by explaining that you are a deviant criminal and not a gentle enlightened man.

Because, no, Nasser, you're not the way to Heaven, just a poor stepping stone to prison or death. I'm sure you know that. You proved it by destroying us, you're a lot smarter than you let on.

However, allow me to offer you a little revelation: you're not as stupid as you like to imply, but you're not as intelligent as one might hope. There's no intelligence where there's no heart. Nor is there intelligence where only the murderer's hatred and hubris prevail. You're cunning, you're subtle despite the ineptitude of your ideology, and you have the charisma to seduce - in the etymological sense of the word, id is to lead astray - men weakened by their existence. Yet tonight, you have lost; and I hope that, even if one day, as is likely, you get out of prison, this book will continue to sing, through the voice of a Muslim woman no less, the victory of national unity over your destructive impulses.

Now you know: when you came to me with your minions, you preached in the desert. Nevertheless, you weren't wrong about everything. As you said, you didn't come to see me by chance. At the time, my colleagues suspected your cowardice: rather than attacking a man, you targeted a woman, reputed to be weaker. I wasn't sure they were right. Today, I'm sure, they were wrong in substance, even if, in form, it was a very nice way for me to say how much they would have liked to get me out of this predicament or face it for me. In reality - Nasser, I implore you to read what follows carefully, as I'm not sure you've verbalized it - you came to see me because you felt I was the one closest to you.

Like you, I'm convinced that I'm different from everyone else.

Like you, I'm convinced that I'm following a path that I hope is the right one, even if I haven't always been able to draw it perfectly straight.

Like you, I believe in Allah.

What makes us different? You decided to enslave and kill your fellow human beings; I chose to fight for human freedom. Ever since we met, I've wanted to spend my life pulling out weeds like yours. But make no mistake, I'm not underestimating you. Your words resonate within me. They fuel my determination to fight relentlessly against fanatics of your ilk. I guess the fight will never be over, so what? Tonight, this first victory over you lights me up with a peaceful joy because, as Rocky Balboa says,

it's not about being a good hitter. The important thing is to get hit and still keep going. It's about being able to take it and never give up. That's how you win.

Can't wait for the next *round*!

Table of contents

Best sellers Max Milo Editions

Hitler's banker, Jean-François Bouchard

Confessions of a forger, Éric Piedoie Le Tiec

The Koran and the flesh, Ludovic-Mohamed Zahed

Governing by fake news, Jacques Baud

Governing by chaos, Collectif

A political history of food, Paul Ariès

Mad in U.S.A.: The ravages of the "American model",
Michel Desmurget

Mondial soccer club geopolitics, Kévin Veyssière

Putin: Game master?, Jacques Braud

Treatise on the three impostors: Moses, Jesus, Muhammad,
The Spirit of Spinoza

TV Lobotomy, Michel Desmurget

www.ingramcontent.com/pod-product-compliance
Lightning Source LLC
LaVergne TN
LVHW051153060726
842526LV00014B/3182